Quarterly Essay

1 THE COAL CURSE
Resources, climate and Australia's future
Judith Brett

83 CORRESPONDENCE
Maryanne Slattery, Mike Young, Stuart Bunn, Gabrielle Chan, Geoff Beeson, Barney Foran, Lauren Rickards, Stefano de Pieri, Peter Gell, Jason Alexandra, R. Humphrey Howie, Margaret Simons

135 Contributors

Quarterly Essay is published four times a year by Black Inc., an imprint of Schwartz Books Pty Ltd. Publisher: Morry Schwartz.

ISBN 9781760642297 ISSN 1832-0953

Subscriptions – 1 year print & digital (4 issues): $79.95 within Australia incl. GST. Outside Australia $119.95. 2 years print & digital (8 issues): $149.95 within Australia incl. GST. 1 year digital only: $49.95.

Payment may be made by Mastercard or Visa, or by cheque made out to Schwartz Books. Payment includes postage and handling.

To subscribe, fill out and post the subscription card or form inside this issue, or subscribe online:

quarterlyessay.com
subscribe@blackincbooks.com
Phone: 61 3 9486 0288

Correspondence should be addressed to:

The Editor, Quarterly Essay
Level 1, 221 Drummond Street
Carlton VIC 3053 Australia
Phone: 61 3 9486 0288 / Fax: 61 3 9011 6106
Email: quarterlyessay@blackincbooks.com

Editor: Chris Feik. Management: Elisabeth Young. Publicity: Anna Lensky. Design: Guy Mirabella. Assistant Editor: Kirstie Innes-Will. Production Coordinator: Marilyn de Castro. Typesetting: Marilyn de Castro.

Printed in Australia by McPherson's Printing Group. The paper used to produce this book comes from wood grown in sustainable forests.

THE COAL CURSE

Resources, climate and Australia's future

Judith Brett

I began writing this essay shortly after Christmas 2019, when south-east Australia was burning and the impacts of climate change were uppermost in everyone's mind. I am finishing it in coronavirus lockdown in May 2020, as we obsessively follow infection and death rates, read endless articles about what to do at home with the kids, worry about the economic mayhem. It's hard to think about anything else. So let me take you back to early January, when the fire fronts were roaring through south-eastern Australia.

On the days around New Year, 4000 people were trapped on the beach at Mallacoota, waiting for the navy to bring in supplies and start an evacuation, car convoys were leaving Bateman's Bay and the other holiday towns on the NSW south coast, Corryong was evacuating to Tallangatta and fire authorities were warning of worse to come. In his press conference the day after New Year, Prime Minister Scott Morrison batted away any suggestion that the catastrophic fires might push the Coalition to go harder on reducing emissions from fossil fuels, with arguments that were all too familiar:

> Our emissions reduction policies will both protect our environment and seek to reduce the risks and hazards we are seeing today. At the

> same time it will seek to ensure the viability of people's jobs and livelihoods all around the country. What we will do is ensure that our policies remain sensible, that they don't move towards either extreme, and stay focused on what Australians need for a vibrant and viable economy, as well as a vibrant and sustainable environment. Getting the balance right is what Australia, I think, has always been able to achieve.

Everything about Morrison's initial response to the fires was wrong, beginning with his ill-considered family holiday in Hawaii, flying off when the fires were already raging and the smoke was so thick in Sydney that tourists couldn't see the Bridge from the Opera House. Morrison was determined to see the fires as part of the expected pattern of Australian summers, and their management as the responsibility of the states' emergency services. After mounting popular outrage forced him to cut his holiday short, he badly misread the reasons for people's anger. He thought his absence had made Australians anxious, as if he were a monarch whose very presence reassured and gave comfort.

It was soon clear his presence was just as likely to arouse anger, and that meet-and-greets with fire victims could not be relied on to provide soothing photo opportunities. Visiting the fire-ravaged village of Cobargo in the Bega Valley, he was heckled, two people refused to shake his hand, and it was filmed for the whole nation to see. What people wanted was not a hug from Scotty, but leadership and decisive action from their prime minister: to pay the volunteer fire-fighters, to make sure they were properly equipped, to provide national leadership and coordination in an emergency that ignored state borders. And they wanted him to talk about climate change, to admit that the ferocity and extent of these fires were what scientists had been predicting as the climate warmed.

Greg Mullins, the former NSW Fire and Rescue Commissioner, described the fires as "unprecedented." In December, he and twenty-eight other former fire and emergency chiefs had called for the prime minister to convene an emergency summit on how the country should prepare for bushfires in a changed climate. Back in April, they had tried to warn Morrison that fire behaviour was changing in Australia, and that a ramped-up and better-coordinated response and more resources were needed. They made a number of practical suggestions, but, said Mullins, "We weren't listened to."

As prime minister, Morrison does not deny that the climate is changing, nor that the burning of fossil fuels is the primary cause. This, it must be said, is a major advance on Tony Abbott's position, which was barely disguised denialism. But Morrison will not admit to the severity of the crisis, nor that his government is failing to respond to its seriousness. In his carefully calibrated statement on 2 January, he balanced two things: cutting emissions and protecting livelihoods "all around the country." Not everyone lived in these fire-prone areas, he was reminding us, some lived in mining regions, and they had interests too, which the government must look after. Here it was again: economy versus environment, and the misleading search for balance between two supposedly competing goods.

As the fires burned, I was in no mood for balance. I was angry. Scientists had been warning of fires like these for decades. Ross Garnaut had predicted fires of this scale in 2008 in the Climate Change Review he authored for state, territory and federal governments. Former fire chiefs had warned of them not twelve months ago, as a persistent drought dried the bush. The government had responded with Dorothea McKellar's land of drought and flooding rains to claim that fires were business-as-usual for the Australian bush and with a childlike theory of causation where the only cause of a fire is the spark that sets it off, whether it be the arsonist's match, the unattended camp fire or a lightning bolt. Of course rising temperatures do not produce the spark, but they do create the conditions to make the fires more intense and destructive. Rainforest was burning that had never burned before, as it had in Tasmania in the first months of 2016.

Over New Year, my favourite place on earth was burned: the campgrounds at Thurra River and Mueller Inlet near the Point Hicks Lighthouse in East Gippsland. I had camped there with family and friends for the past twenty years, and we were booked to camp there again in February. It was beautiful: magnificent old mahogany gums with snaking trunks and limbs, a short tannin-bronzed river and estuary, long white beaches and sheltered bays, enormous sand dunes which took you to the top of the world. For a few weeks a year it was all ours, as so many annual holiday spots on the south and east coasts are to others.

I know that the loss of a loved camping ground is not in the same league as burned houses, sheds and livestock, or a loved friend or family member killed fighting the fire. We weren't there and we didn't face the horror of the walls of flame. Our comfortable city-based lives went on almost as usual. But awake at night I had losses to mourn: the habitat destruction, and the reptiles, birds and animals that had been killed – the stately lace monitors, the lyrebirds and red-bellied black snakes, the bright blue dragonflies. Maybe it will all bounce back; but maybe it won't. Maybe it will be burned again before the plants and animals have the chance to recover. It is not just the intensity of the fires that is new, but their increased frequency, and both will get worse as the planet heats.

Over the summer, Australia's international reputation took a hammering as the world's media filled with apocalyptic images of kilometre-high flames, fleeing kangaroos and burnt koalas, a small boy in a boat on a wine-dark sea, devastated communities and cities smothered in smoke. As we watched, fresh in many minds was the shameful performance of Energy Minister Angus Taylor at the UN-convened climate conference in Madrid in December, which had aimed to ratchet up the global effort to reduce emissions.

Before countries could agree to higher targets, the rules needed to be sorted out. In particular, should countries be allowed to carry over as credits towards meeting their Paris targets any overshoot in achieving the reductions they committed to at Kyoto? Australia argued they should. Australia had negotiated an easy target for itself at Kyoto by including changes to land-clearing laws. Now it wanted to use that easy target to reduce the effort needed to meet its Paris targets. Many other countries also had credits, but none planned to use them to meet their targets and most explicitly ruled this out as an accounting ploy which avoided the real task of cutting emissions.

With carry-over credits from Kyoto, Australia easily reaches its Paris target of a 26 per cent cut in emissions from 2005. Without them the reduction would only be 16 per cent, and we would have almost to double our efforts to meet the target. Carry-over credits were not allowed under the Paris Agreement, and developing countries lobbied hard against them being allowed at Madrid. Taylor, though, was intransigent, so a decision on how to treat them was kicked down the road to the next conference, which was to be held in Glasgow in November 2020, but has now been postponed due to the COVID-19 pandemic.

Australia once prided itself on being a good international citizen, a middle-ranking power that could punch above its weight in debates on matters of global importance. Once, we cared what other countries thought of us. The high point of our reputation was 1988 to 1996, when Gareth Evans was Australia's foreign minister and made major contributions to the peace process in Cambodia, the control of chemical weapons and the formation of APEC. But since the Howard government refused to allow the captain of Norwegian vessel MV *Tampa* to land rescued asylum seekers in Australia, our cruel treatment of refugees arriving by sea has forfeited much of this reputation. Playing the spoiler in global climate negotiations is shredding what's left.

On his return from Madrid, as the fires raged, Taylor wrote an article for *The Australian* arguing that we "should be proud of our climate change efforts" and repeating the claim that we are "responsible for only 1.3 per cent of global emissions, so we can't single-handedly have a meaningful impact without the co-operation of the largest emitters such as China and the US." Because international targets are based on domestic emissions, Taylor did not include emissions from the fossil fuels we export in the form of coal and liquefied natural gas. Add these in, and we become responsible for 3.6 per cent of the world's emissions. China, the United States and India are the world's biggest emitters, but their populations are much larger. Per capita, our emissions are second in the world, only slightly less than Saudi Arabia's.

The rest of the world sees no reason for Australia to be proud of its climate change efforts. After the Madrid conference, Australia was widely identified as one of a small number of countries wrecking the chance of effective global agreements to cut emissions. UN Secretary-General Antonio Guterres said, "The international community lost an important opportunity to show increased ambition on mitigation, adaptation and finance to tackle the climate crisis."

Although the government was refusing to link the fires to climate change, to the rest of the world the connections between climate, coal and the fires were obvious, as was the motivation for the government's obfuscation. On 20 December, the Friday before Christmas, when Australia was the hottest place in the world, Ros Atkins of BBC News stood in front of a map showing fires all down the east coast and over much of the rest of the country. The impacts of global warming, which scientists had predicted, had arrived, he said, yet admitting this was politically controversial for the government because fossil fuels, coal in particular, are a major export industry for Australia.

Writing in *The Atlantic* a fortnight later, Robinson Meyer described Australia as "caught in a climate spiral."

> For the past few decades, the arid and affluent country of 25 million has padded out its economy – otherwise dominated by sandy beaches and a bustling service sector – by selling coal to the world … But now Australia is buckling under the conditions that its fossil fuels have helped bring about.

It is not just our reputation that is at stake. As global concern escalates about the devastating impacts of climate change, there are risks to our trade. In November 2019, the French foreign minister, Jean-Yves Le Drian, warned the Morrison government that a planned free trade deal between Australia and the European Union must incorporate ambitious action on climate change.

The European Commission is committed to reaching net zero carbon emissions by 2050. At the World Economic Forum's Annual Meeting at Davos in January, its new president, Ursula von der Leyen, made it clear that the EU intended to impose a carbon tax on imports from countries that do not support international climate goals, both to accelerate global action and to protect its own industries from a competitive disadvantage when dealing with recalcitrant global polluters. While this is not yet EU policy, it is not in Australia's long-term interests to be labelled a recalcitrant global polluter.

Australia has been cursed with a decade of poor national leadership on climate change, with our prime ministers lacking either the intellect or the courage to develop coherent policy responses to the threat. Much has been written on the sorry litany of failed attempts: Rudd's squibbing of the greatest moral challenge of our time; Gillard's bumbling over whether or not the emissions reduction scheme was a tax; Abbott's ruthless exploitation of her blunder and the Coalition's weaponising of climate change; Turnbull's inability to face down the climate deniers in his party; the pernicious role of the Murdoch press in undermining Labor's modest efforts; the fact that we still don't have a workable energy policy.

Pushed by city Liberals who understand the urgency of the problem and fear for their seats as their electorates run out of patience, Morrison now talks of balance, which at least acknowledges that the climate is changing. But there is still a rump of deniers on the government's back bench, mainly Nationals, who resist any move to set higher targets for emissions cuts, no matter how small the increase, and want the government to invest in a coal-fired power station in Queensland, even though this makes little economic sense. Speaking in February 2020, Malcom Turnbull likened the climate change deniers in the Liberal Party to terrorists, willing to blow the joint up to hold their ground. He should know. But just as important are the climate change minimisers: those who admit the world is warming but say we have plenty of time to respond and who worry about the economic disruption of acting too fast.

How has Australia ended up here? How did climate change denial gain such a deadly grip on our political class? I have written this essay in an attempt to do something constructive with my grief and anger, and my fear for our collective future; not just to fume and blame, but to try to understand.

I am a historian, so I look for explanations not just in the perfidies of the present, but in the decisions and events of the past. Social scientists talk about "path dependence": the way established institutions and ways of doing things shape present actions and future possibilities. This is just a fancy way of saying that history matters, but it does shift our attention from the contingencies of events and personalities to structures and institutions. This essay is about the history of Australia as a commodity-exporting nation and its political consequences. Economic history is unfashionable nowadays. Economists focus on the modelling and management of the present and historians are more interested in stories and experience, and in uncovering diversity and neglected voices. Economic history is dry and hard to narrativise. But how a country makes its living can explain a lot.

In 2018–19, Australia's top exports were iron ore, coal, natural gas, international education and tourism, in that order. Coal became our top-earning export commodity in the mid-1980s and has been at number one or number two ever since, vying with iron ore, which needs metallurgical coal to be transformed into steel. The production of LNG has increased rapidly over the past decade since the massive developments in Gladstone, Queensland, and it is now our third-largest commodity export and rising fast. Between 2018–19 and the previous financial year, its export value grew by 60.9 per cent. Coal, LNG, iron ore: in 2018–19 these three earned 41.8 per cent of our export income.

This is why Morrison brought a lump of lacquered Hunter Valley coal into parliament in February 2017. "Don't be afraid, don't be scared, it won't hurt you," he said, as he handed it along the grinning front bench, "it's coal." The point was to ridicule the Opposition's support for renewable energy, and it was a stupid stunt. But it put on full display how impossible it was for many of our political leaders to imagine Australia's future without fossil fuels. Australia is the world's second-largest exporter of coal, and in 2019 we overtook Qatar to become the largest exporter of LNG. So we are now the world's third-largest exporter of fossil fuels, behind only Saudi Arabia and Russia.

Australia is a trading nation. We have a small population, so exporting enables our companies to grow by reaching larger markets. We need the foreign income earned by our exports to pay for the goods and services we import, and to service debts to foreign lenders. Our exporters also contribute to the national economy by paying taxes, distributing dividends to shareholders and employing people. All this is true of the fossil-fuel exporters, but there are costs to having an export profile so skewed to one sector.

The term "resource curse" was first used by the British economist Richard Auty in 1993 to explain why some resource-rich countries suffer from slow development and corrupt, authoritarian political elites: for example, Nigeria, Angola, Venezuela. At worst, the country embarks on a spending spree, using the export income earned to buy expensive imports, and is left with little when the limited resources run out, as happened most notoriously to Nauru. For a few decades, the money flowed from its phosphate deposits, but when the phosphate ran out, the economy collapsed.

The idea of the resource curse is highly contested, and a country's institutions are crucial in preventing the worst outcomes. A strong civil society, functioning democratic institutions and the rule of law can limit corruption and underpin a functioning diverse economy like Australia's. We will turn to the political effects of the resource curse on Australia later in this essay. On the economic effects, not all economists see a country's reliance on natural resources to earn export income as a problem. They argue that a country should pursue its comparative advantage and if that is in the production of natural resources, then that is what they should sell to the world, buying manufactured goods from countries that can produce them more efficiently.

Australia has a comparative advantage in mineral and agricultural commodities, and exporting these has made us rich. But trade in unprocessed commodities has some significant disadvantages compared with trade in manufactured goods. First, it is a declining sector of world trade. In the nineteenth century, commodity trade was two-thirds of all world trade; by 1966 it was one-third; and by 1983, it had halved again to 17 per cent. The main game in global trade is in manufactured goods, so no matter how strong our performance as an exporter of minerals, we are locked into a declining sector of world trade.

Second, until recently, world commodity prices were falling relative to manufactured goods, although the explosion of cheap Chinese manufacturing since the start of the twenty-first century has reversed this, with a dramatic fall in the price of manufactured goods. Third, the price of manufactured goods has historically been more stable than the fluctuating commodity prices, so the export income they earn has been more reliable and the economies of manufacturing countries less vulnerable to external shocks. In Australia, the depression of the early 1890s and the Great Depression of the 1930s were both partly caused by precipitous falls in the price of wool.

As a commodity-exporting, manufactured goods–importing country, Australia has had recurring problems with its terms of trade, which is the ratio between the prices of exports and imports; in simple terms, how many bales of wool and container loads of coal we must export to pay for the motor vehicles, computers and clothes we import.

Booms in commodity prices can be just as destabilising as busts. Resource booms push up the value of a country's currency, which makes it harder for other exporters to sell to the world. They also draw capital and labour from other sectors of the economy in pursuit of better returns and higher wages. The discovery of gold in Victoria in the early 1850s emptied Adelaide of able-bodied men almost overnight. The fly-in, fly-out work to build the infrastructure for the recent resources boom has lured workers, especially skilled tradespeople, away from cities and regional towns. Jobs created by a booming commodities sector must be balanced against those lost elsewhere. This is sometimes called the "Dutch disease," a term first used in 1977 by *The Economist* to explain the effect the Netherlands' exploitation of North Sea oil and gas had on the rest of its economy, especially manufacturing, which shrank.

Harvard University's Center for International Development has an Atlas of Economic Complexity, which ranks economies according to their diversity and complexity in order to assess their potential for growth. In 2017, Australia came in at number 93 of 133 economies ranked according to the diversity and complexity of exports. Our neighbours on the scale were Senegal and Pakistan. Above and below us were underdeveloped, non-Western countries, those we once called "third world." The nearest country we like to compare ourselves with was New Zealand, at 51. All the other OECD countries were well above us, with Japan leading the way at number one.

And the picture gets worse. Australia is slipping down the ranks, falling twenty-three places in the past decade. Other countries with falls of similar magnitude were Zimbabwe, Cuba and Zambia; the reasons were political instability and civil war, and an increasing dependence on the export of commodities. We have had some political instability, but the main culprit for our decline is the resources boom that began in 2003. It made us rich, but it also increased our reliance on selling the world what we dig up.

The Harvard Atlas takes the total diversity of a country's exports as an expression of its collective knowledge and sees this as the basis for future growth. It places the complexity of "the industrial capabilities of a country at the heart of its growth prospects." From this perspective, we are a dumb country with a weak industrial base and poor prospects. The *Australian Financial Review* headed its report on the Harvard index, "Australia is rich, dumb and getting dumber."

The problem is not so much what we sell to the world, but what we don't sell: a diverse range of capital-intensive, value-added industrial products that require high levels of specific knowledge and skills. Just over 7 per cent of us work in manufacturing. Of these 923,300 people, fewer than 80,000 are skilled metal workers: 42,500 structural steel workers and welders and 36,400 metal fitters and machinists. The bulk of our manufacturing workers are in ancillary roles, such as sale managers and packers, or in low value–added food processing.

The Harvard Atlas overstates how dumb we are. Until COVID-19 disrupted global travel, our fourth-largest earner of foreign income was education and related services and our fifth was tourism. We lead the world in much of our mining and metallurgical technology, and our international education is bigger proportionately than anywhere else. But in 2018–19, seven of our top ten exports were from the quarry and one from the farm. Here they are in order: iron ores and concentrates, coal, natural gas, education-related travel services, personal travel except education, gold, aluminium ores and concentrates, beef, crude petroleum, copper ores and concentrates.

Historically, the biggest problem with Australia's efficient production of primary commodities has been that it did not produce enough jobs for the nation we aspired to be. It didn't when we were the world's largest exporter of wool, and it doesn't now. Despite all that we hear from our politicians about jobs in mining, they are comparatively few: currently only around 1.9 per cent of the workforce, and set to fall further as the big miners automate more functions. As Chris Salisbury, Rio Tinto's iron ore chief executive, put it, "For mining companies the key focus is to control the controllables." Big swings in the global price for iron ore are not controllable, but labour costs are. Salisbury has recently overseen the development of AutoHaul, Rio Tinto's fully automated heavy-haul long-distance rail network for its Western Australian iron ore mines. Dubbed the world's largest robots, 2.4-kilometre-long driverless trains take the ore from mine to port. Unsurprisingly, since AutoHaul was implemented, there are fewer industrial accidents, because there are fewer workers to injure.

Similarly, Adani has now retreated from initial claims that its Carmichael coalmine would create 10,000 jobs to the far more modest 1464, a figure that includes indirect jobs and takes into account the loss of jobs in other mines caused by Carmichael's operations. Under oath, Adani's own economist said of the impact of the project in the Queensland Land Court: "It's not many jobs. We can agree on that."

Across the nation, there are not many jobs in coalmining at all: 35,638 in June 2018. By comparison, in 2013, the year before Joe Hockey and Tony Abbott closed down Australia's car industry, about 44,000 people in Australia were employed in the manufacture of cars, engines, electrical and other components, as well as trucks, buses and products for the automotive after-market.

Farmers, fishers and foresters, the workers in the other sector producing primary commodities, are also few, at around 2.5 per cent of the workforce. So if we add this to the 1.9 per cent from mining, 4.4 per cent of our workers are in the industries that produce almost 70 per cent of our export income.

The usual trajectory of economic development is the transfer of resources from low-productivity agriculture to higher-productivity manufacturing. This is the transition Britain undertook in the Industrial Revolution, Japan after the Meiji restoration of 1868, Germany after its unification, South Korea in the 1950s, and which is currently underway in India and China. Capital moves from agriculture into manufacturing; peasants leave the fields for the factories, where their labour is more productive and they can earn more money; the cities grow in wealth and political influence; and modern industrial societies develop. Australia has not followed this trajectory.

In the 1980s and 1990s, it seemed that our exports might diversify, that we might become less reliant on a handful of top earners. It didn't happen. We are still a country that depends overwhelmingly on the export of a few primary commodities shipped to the world raw and requiring very few of us to produce. How did this happen?

FROM WOOL TO IRON, COAL AND GAS

Like so much else in our history, the story begins with wool. Australia is rich in resources. Nature's gifts have provided the foundation for our prosperity since the early decades of the nineteenth century, when John Macarthur and his wife, Elizabeth, discovered how to breed merino sheep on Australia's grasslands to supply Britain with fine wool. Gold followed from the 1850s, luring adventurous young immigrants with dreams of easy fortunes and building inland cities, such as Ballarat and Bendigo in Victoria, Gympie in Queensland, and Kalgoorlie in Western Australia. The mid-century immigrants also laid the foundations for Australia's successful democracy, with near universal male franchise, compulsory free education and the world's first eight-hour day.

Growing rich in the nineteenth century from the export of primary commodities set up a dual structure in the Australian economy that persists to this day, with an outward-looking export sector employing few people and a domestic sector where most people work but which contributes far less to our export income. There are two stories here: the first about our success in exporting commodities and the second about the weakness of our industrialisation, which failed to develop manufactured goods for export.

First, the success story. Australia became one of the world's wealthiest countries in the nineteenth century because it had plentiful land to graze sheep and a ready market in Britain's woollen mills. Wool made pastoralists phenomenally rich, but it also built the wealth of the coastal capital cities as commercial centres and ports through which wool was shipped from rural hinterlands to world markets. In the early twentieth century, rural exports diversified to include wheat, dairy, meat and sugar, but wool remained king.

Australia rode on the sheep's back until the 1950s. It was the world's largest producer of wool; and before World War II wool provided around a third of export income. In 1950, when US demand for uniforms for the

Korean War pushed up the price, wool earned almost 50 per cent. This high didn't last. The Korean War ended, but more significantly, artificial fibres started to erode wool's markets and drive down its price. Australia is still the world's largest producer of wool, but it now earns less than 1 per cent of our export income.

Fortuitously for Australia, as wool was in freefall, the export of minerals began to rise, spurred by post-war demand for uranium and the new metals of aluminium, tungsten and titanium. Uranium deposits were discovered at Rum Jungle and at Jabiru, both close to Darwin, but export success was short-lived. These discoveries did, however, draw the attention of mineral prospectors to Australia's tropical north. This was a disaster with far-reaching consequences for many Indigenous communities in northern Australia, especially after huge deposits of bauxite were found in the Gulf of Carpentaria. Subsequently, bauxite deposits were also found in south-east Western Australia, close to Perth. Australia is now the world's largest producer of bauxite. Bauxite is refined into alumina, which is then smelted into aluminium, and both refineries and smelters were established in regional towns.

Oil exploration intensified after the war, leading eventually to the discovery and development of the oil fields in Bass Strait, but Australia is small fry in oil. The other really big mineral discovery in the 1950s was made by pastoralist Lang Hancock. Flying his plane lower than usual through the Hamersley Range in the Pilbara, he noticed the rusty colour of oxidised iron on the walls of the gorge of the Turner River.

In 1938, with war looming, the Lyons government had embargoed the export of iron ore, believing Australia's supplies to be limited. As well, the Western Australian government was refusing to grant titles to explore for iron ore and did not guarantee that successful prospectors could exploit their discoveries. So Hancock kept his discovery quiet, but lobbied for the lifting of the embargo and the changing of the licensing laws. With Japan's appetite for iron ore growing and Australia needing to find new sources of export income, the federal government began to relax the embargo in 1960 and the transformation of the Pilbara into one of the world's great resource provinces began. Within little more than a decade, a string of iron ports ran along the north-west coast, from Geraldton to Darwin, joined by railway lines to large open-cut mines in the interior.

The timing was good. Since the first bales of wool were loaded onto sailing ships, Britain had been the major destination for Australia's exports. But Britain was about to dump us and our sister Commonwealth countries for the European Common Market (now the European Union). The French president, Charles de Gaulle, vetoed Britain's first and second attempts to join, but it was only a matter of time. Australia had to find new markets fast. Our saviour was industrialising Japan and its demand for iron ore to make steel. In 1963–64, Britain was still our top export destination, but by 1967 it was Japan, which remained our leading market until overtaken by China in 2009–10.

In two significant ways Australia's trade with the world looked very different in 1980 from 1950. Minerals had replaced pastoral and agricultural products as our leading exports, and Asia had replaced the United Kingdom and Europe as our main market. In one significant way, though, our trade had stayed the same: we were still shipping unprocessed commodities to the world. And this was about to intensify as coal became a major export.

Australia had been exporting small quantities of coal since the nineteenth century, but most was used domestically, for transport, heating and electricity generation, and as coking coal to make steel. Our abundance of coal gave us cheap energy, which was a major boost to our development. Only recently has it become an export staple.

Mining companies were hungry for new fields. The most promising was the Galilee Basin, which had remained unmined because of its distance from the sea and the expense of infrastructure needed to reach it. The higher price changed the calculations. Claims to mine the basin were staked, including most notoriously by the Indian magnate Gautam Adani, but also by Australia's very own billionaires Gina Rinehart and Clive Palmer. Similarly, miners were lining up to expand coalmining in the nearby Bowen Basin and to exploit its gas reserves, as well as in the Surat Basin, which extends south into northern New South Wales.

Australia mines three types of coal: brown, and two types of black – thermal and metallurgical, or coking, coal. Brown coal is not exported but used for domestic power generation, especially in Victoria's La Trobe Valley. It is the most carbon-polluting of the three types and is being phased out as the aging power stations that burn it, like Hazelwood in Victoria, reach their use-by dates and are closed down. Thermal coal is also burned to keep Australia's lights on, and the climate deniers want this to continue. As of 2012, Australia had the fifth-largest known deposits of black coal in the world, a little more than 9 per cent of the total. These deposits are mostly in the Hunter Valley and Liverpool Plains in New South Wales and in the Bowen and Galilee basins in central Queensland. The coal we export is both thermal and metallurgical. The thermal coal is used to generate electricity. Metallurgical coal is transformed into the coke used in the blast furnaces that turn iron ore into steel.

Since the early 1990s, Australia's production and export of coal has grown exponentially, driven largely by the industrialisation of Asian countries, and more recently by galloping demand from China. During the 1980s, Australia produced less than a hundred million toe of coal a year (toe is a unit of energy which means ton of oil equivalent). This rose to 150 million toe a year by 1996, 250 million by 2010 and, after a short blip due to the global financial crisis, rocketed up to around 300 million per annum by 2013, where it has mostly stayed. As well, port and rail expansions were underway to get the coal to market.

The impact of the coal rush was magnified by changes in the way coal is mined. The deep mines and coal pits of the past have been replaced with open-cut mega-mines, which strip the vegetation and topsoil and compete with agriculture for access to the land. For people living in these areas, it was like being run over by a bus – or in this case a train of coal carts.

*

In the early 2000s, another resource joined the ranks of our top exports: liquefied coalseam gas. In the 1980s, the company Woodside discovered huge deposits of natural gas, mostly methane, off the north-west coast of Western Australia. In the past, gas was difficult to transport, so it could only be used close to its source, but with new technologies the gas could be liquefied, stored and transported. Large plants were built to liquefy it and Australia had a new export commodity.

The first cargo of north-west shelf LNG left for Japan in 1989 on a ship named the *Northwest Sanderling*, after a small wading bird that makes an annual migration from the Arctic to the shores of Australia, transiting in Japan. Woodside must have had a twitcher in its management, for later ships were also named after migratory birds – snipe, shearwater, sandpiper – to symbolise the linking of an Australian resource with a reliable Japanese market. By 2012, 3000 shiploads of LNG had been carried to Japan, and by 2013 Australia was the world's third-largest LNG exporter.

In 2015, LNG exports began on the other side of the continent, from Curtis Island off the coast north of Gladstone. Three newly built plants liquefied coal-seam gas, which was shipped from newly built port facilities to customers in Asia. Bechtel, the lucky firm that got the construction contracts, said it was "the largest concentration of private-capital investment in Australia's history." We are now the world's largest LNG exporter. But because the industry overestimated the amount of available gas, and governments failed to insist that some be reserved for domestic use, prices for households and businesses skyrocketed. Domestic supplies were raided to meet export contracts, and by 2017 Australians were paying the highest gas prices in the developed world.

Exporting minerals and gas has saved Australia since global demand for wool collapsed, but it has continued the massive disconnect between the section of the economy that earns most of the export income and the one that creates most of the jobs. The second story we need to understand our dependence on the export of fossil fules is about Australia's weak industrialisation.

As a new settler society, modern Australia had plentiful land, stolen from the Indigenous population and lush with grass. It was also unencumbered by traditional European agricultural methods. With no old men shaking their heads at newfangled ideas, new livestock breeds and farming techniques spread rapidly. From a strictly economic point of view, Australia might have developed as an efficient agricultural economy with a small population. But this was never politically feasible. Colonial Australians wanted a modern, economically developed nation with a large population. Agriculture would never create enough jobs for the nation they aspired to create, and economic development meant industrialisation.

Australia has made successive efforts to industrialise. The first was in colonial Victoria in the 1860s. In the decade after gold was discovered in 1851, Victoria's population increased by 450 per cent. Some immigrants made it rich on the diggings, but most didn't, and as the gold ran out they needed to make a living. Many wanted land of their own and campaigned to unlock the pastoralists' vast holdings to provide family farms. Others wanted protective tariffs to encourage manufacturing, which would provide jobs and build the cities.

Australia's earliest popularly based political party was the National Reform and Protection League, formed to fight the 1877 Victorian election. A broad alliance of miners, small farmers, manufacturers and trade unionists, its key demands were a land tax to induce the subdivision of large estates, extension of a protective tariff, and reform of Victoria's conservative upper house so it couldn't block these radical measures. The League's leader, the fiery Graham Berry, became premier.

Berry was a convinced protectionist, as were other Victorian colonial liberals, like *Age* editor David Syme and politician Alfred Deakin. It was a deeply felt issue. Protectionists were breaking with a sacred tenet of classical British liberalism: belief in free trade. This had been cemented by the campaign against Britain's corn laws during the 1840s, when many of

Australia's young immigrants were forming their political views. The corn laws protected landowners from cheap imported grain and preserved their economic and political power. They also increased the price of the dietary staple, bread, and slowed the growth of manufacturing. After they had fed themselves and their families, most people had little spare money to spend on the clothes and household goods being produced in the mills and potteries of the midlands.

Free trade became associated with a fair and open society, and protection with inflated prices and vested interests. Colonial circumstances were different, argued men like Berry and Syme. John Stuart Mill, the doyen of English liberals, had made an exception for the temporary imposition of tariffs "in a young and rising nation" to allow industries to develop. He stipulated, though, that these should be temporary, and that domestic producers should not expect them to continue indefinitely. Alfred Deakin describes crossing the fiscal Rubicon from his immigrant father's faith in free trade to a belief in the virtues of protection, persuaded by Syme while they walked together across the old Princes Bridge. To Syme, free trade meant monopoly for the British manufacturers and prevented the fledgling colony from developing its own economy and society.

By the 1880s, protection was entrenched policy in Victoria. Not so across the Murray in New South Wales. Colonial government used tariffs on imports to raise revenue. The question was, should they also be used as an instrument of industrial progress? New South Wales had no sudden need to find jobs for a rush of men, and protective tariffs would harm its established export-oriented industries of pastoralism and coal, so it stayed committed to free trade.

As is well known, the colonies' differences over trade slowed the progress of federation, but protection won the day. Under the New Protection of the twentieth century's first decade, an alliance was formed between manufacturers, who would be protected from imports, and workers, who would be paid higher wages from the profits made possible by protection. Primary producers were not happy. Tariffs increased their costs, especially the prices they had to pay for machinery, and these could not be passed on to price-sensitive overseas buyers. Eventually, though, they joined the game. It was to be "protection all round" when, after 1920, the newly formed Country Party lobbied for bounties and marketing schemes to protect the incomes of rural producers.

Crucially, Australia's protected manufacturers were making products for the home market, not for export. The goal was import substitution. Australians would buy Australian-made clothes and household goods; governments would buy Australian-made trains, trams and stationery; farmers would buy Australian-made ploughs and harvesters. The cities certainly earned good income from the raw products passing through their ports to world markets, but much of their economic activity was providing goods and services to their inhabitants: building, furnishing and decorating houses, shops and public buildings; feeding, clothing, grooming and entertaining; transporting goods and people; providing medical, educational, financial, legal and spiritual services, and so on. The cities were also the seats of government, creating employment in public administration.

The nascent nineteenth-century manufacturing sector looked inward to the domestic market, not outward to the world. This might not have been a problem had the population been larger, like that of the United States, but the home market was small. Consequently, our industrialisation was inefficient, unable to exploit the economies of scale available in larger markets, and it was defensive, relying for its survival on tariffs rather than on price or quality.

By the time of federation, Australia's distinctive pattern of population was well established. A third of its population of almost 4 million lived in the coastal capitals, a proportion that increased steadily as the century progressed. By 1945 it was half, and in 2016 it was two-thirds. Despite its large landmass and outdoor image, Australia is one of the world's most urbanised nations. Almost 90 per cent of us live in urban areas and these are the favoured destinations of new immigrants, who guarantee increased demand each year as they establish their households. Our cities have a self-sustaining economic momentum.

The combination of an export-oriented commodity sector with protected, domestically focused manufacturing set up a dual structure in the Australian economy. Our mining and agricultural producers were exposed to a competitive and uncertain world market. To survive, they needed to be resilient and adaptive. Competition made them efficient. Centred outside the capital cities in the regions, they did not employ very many people. In fact, the fewer people they employed, the more internationally competitive they became. Our protected manufacturing sector provided jobs for the largely urban population. But it was inefficient, insulated from global competition, dependent for innovation on imported R&D, and with high costs for both labour and equipment, developing against the economic logic of a small and rich agricultural economy at considerable distance from world markets.

After federation, Australian manufacturing capacity developed slowly, with a burst of activity in the 1920s when the first car was assembled. In 1925, Ford opened a large factory in Geelong, and General Motors followed in Adelaide a year later. As well as providing employment, it was hoped that car manufacturing would encourage metal-based manufacturing more generally and make Australia more self-sufficient. By 1939, manufacturing was contributing 19 per cent to GDP, almost equal to the rural sector's 20 per cent.

The war turbo-charged Australia's manufacturing. The disruption of shipping routes boosted protection of domestic firms and the federal government redirected labour and capital to make the goods necessary to wage war: guns, bullets, ships, aircraft, tanks, heavy lorries and so on. By 1940–41, manufacturing's share of employment was 25 per cent and had overtaken the rural sector's share.

Cooperation with the Allies increased Australian access to advanced technology. The economic historian Boris Schedvin judges that Australian industry was most competitive and technologically advanced in the late 1940s.

The war had another major impact on Australian manufacturing. It encouraged a new round of protection to create industries to employ a new wave of immigrants. The war with Japan had left policy-makers anxious about the vulnerability of Australia's small population. The Labor government initiated an ambitious migration program, which the Menzies government continued. The slogan was "Populate or perish," as Australia looked beyond its traditional sources of migration in the British Isles to displaced persons from northern and eastern Europe, and later to the young workers of the Mediterranean, Yugoslavia and the Middle East. These new migrants would need jobs, which would be provided by expanding manufacturing, which in turn would be created by inviting foreign investors to build factories behind tariff walls. Foreign firms would bring their capital and technology and the government would provide workers and a protected domestic market.

Migration, foreign investment and protection combined to create a greatly expanded Australian manufacturing sector in the decades after World War II. In the late 1950s and early 1960s, it peaked at just under 30 per cent of GDP. This was the golden age of Australian protectionism, and it served its primary purpose of providing jobs for the new migrants so that they would settle permanently in Australia. But it did not build an enduring industrial sector. Manufacturing is now only around 6 per cent of GDP.

While Australia was strengthening its tariff walls, other developed countries were dismantling theirs. Protection had increased during the 1930s, as governments struggled to manage the effects of the Depression, and this was widely believed to have contributed to the international tensions that had led to World War II. The 1947 General Agreement on Tariffs and Trade (GATT) aimed at a freer system, with its prime focus on trade in manufactured goods. Australia's exports were almost entirely agricultural, with minimal trade in manufactured goods, so it was permitted to retain and expand its protective policies. This cut Australia off from the phenomenal growth of trade in manufactured goods in the decades after the war.

Protection could have been used to develop manufactured goods for Australia to export. But this is not what happened. Instead, behind our tariff wall we developed a miniature replica economy in which consumers had a choice of Australian-made refrigerators, wirelesses, clothes and so on, all costing more than if they were imported. Small domestic markets severely limited efficiencies of scale, especially when customers were given a choice. Take cars. By the 1970s, four companies built cars here, and another three assembled them from imported kits. Such a fragmented market with short production runs would never produce the economies of scale required to produce goods for export in a competitive global market. The dependence of manufacturing on foreign investment also inhibited the growth of manufacturing exports. Australia was a branch plant economy. Why would head office in Detroit or Tokyo want to encourage the manufacture of cars here to compete with itself in world markets?

It could have been different. Some countries with small populations adopted another strategy. Instead of spreading their manufacturing capacity over a range of products and giving priority to consumer choice, they specialised in a few products for a world market. Sweden, with a population only a little over 10 million, has developed a successful export-oriented, high-tech industrial sector. In 2016, this sector accounted for 77 per cent of the total value of Swedish exports. Volvo is a global brand; no Australian-produced car ever was.

Protection made local management lazy, with a firm's survival depending more on its success in maintaining tariffs than on pursuing competitive advantage. Sheltered from competition with the world's best practice, firms were under less pressure to innovate. Foreign-owned companies imported technology and management practices from head office; local research and development was minimal. John Stuart Mill was naive to think that tariffs could be easily dismantled, as they created vested interests that would lobby for their continuation. Playing golf with a member of the Tariff Board could do more for a firm's future prosperity than overseeing the development of a new product.

In *The Lucky Country*, published in 1964, Donald Horne described Australia's regime of tariff protection as producing "a look-no-brains attitude": "The processes of invention and innovation that are such an essential part of the Western Mind play less domestic part in Australia than in any other prosperous country, apart from Canada." He went on to speculate that Australia's economic derivativeness was making us "a stupid society, a childish society that is self-confident with the familiar and uncomfortable with the unfamiliar, not capable of reacting to danger or making its own decisions." Much has changed in Australia since the 1960s, but this is a good description of the way sections of our elites have responded to climate change, ignoring the risks to stick with what they know. She'll be right, mate – until she won't.

Horne was not alone in criticising protection in the early 1960s. In 1965, the Menzies government commissioned a report by John Vernon into the management of the Australian economy which raised doubts about its long-term wisdom. These were welcomed by anti-tariff campaigner and Liberal backbencher Bert Kelly: "How often have we been slapping protection around just to create employment, forgetting all the while that we were harming employment and development in other industries and, in particular, damaging their export potential ... As we become more industrialised, we shall have to be more instead of less careful about how we use the tariff weapon." There was no chance in the mid-1960s of Kelly's views gaining traction with the political class. Later, after the Liberal Party embraced free trade, the "Modest Member," as he called himself, became a Coalition hero.

Tariff levels were set by a statutory authority, the Tariff Board, which advised the government on the levels of protection needed to encourage "economic and efficient" industries. What this meant was not spelt out and levels tended to be based on precedent. John McEwen, the granite-faced leader of the Country Party, was Minister for Trade. As a returned serviceman, he remained wedded to the nation-building goals of post-war migration and industry development and opposed to reducing tariffs, even though these disadvantaged his trade-exposed rural constituents. In the 1960s, tariffs averaged 46 per cent, with some as high as 120 per cent.

Under chairman Alf Rattigan, in 1967 the Board proposed a systematic review of tariffs, which the government rejected after energetic lobbying from manufacturers. Commerce and farm lobby groups supported Rattigan, as did some academics and the majority of economics writers in the daily press, but nothing happened until Gough Whitlam won office for Labor in 1972. In July the following year, an across-the-board 25 per cent reduction of all tariffs was announced.

These Whitlam government initiatives are now seen as the first tentative steps in the deregulation of the Australian economy. At the time, the main motivation was to reduce the current account surplus to dampen inflation and many regarded them as irresponsible – just what you would expect when inexperienced Labor men got their hands on the reins of government. The long post-war boom was ending. As the economy deteriorated and unemployment rose, Labor's opponents pointed to the tariff reductions as a prime contributor. The Whitlam government was dismissed at the end of 1975. Under the new Coalition government with Malcolm Fraser as prime minister, manufacturers, state governments and unions all lobbied to strengthen protection. Over the next six years, assistance to the clothing and footwear and the motor vehicle and parts industries was massively increased. These were big employers but were requiring ever higher levels of protection to stay afloat as manufacturing capacity shifted from the West to Asia. Fully imported cars, for example, had a tariff of 57.5 per cent as well as quotas on how many could be brought into the country.

By the time Labor came to office in 1983, elite opinion was shifting fast from the protectionist policies that had held sway in Australia since federation. Western governments faced a combination of high unemployment and high inflation, which were not meant to occur together, as unemployment was caused by too little demand and inflation by too much. Policymakers were looking for new ways to understand what was happening.

The result was neoliberalism, with its core argument that governments had grown too large and were interfering with the market's rational distribution of resources. The neoliberal solution was to shift resources from the public to the private sector using a range of strategies: cutting government spending, privatising public enterprises, dismantling government regulations. Support for neoliberal ideas was building inside the Liberal Party, but Fraser was not convinced. Nor, after the Dismissal, did he have the political capital to undertake difficult reforms. It was Labor that would do the heavy lifting in deregulating the Australian economy and opening it to the world.

Led by the charismatic ex-president of the ACTU, Bob Hawke, Labor won the 1983 election and governed for the next thirteen years, restructuring the economy while at the same time implementing social democratic reforms such as Medicare and the Accord, which kept a floor under minimum wages. Its first shock economic move was to float the Australian dollar and open up the finance and banking sector. No longer would the government have to balance the competing interests of exporters, manufacturers and domestic consumers when setting the official exchange rate. Instead, the international capital market would decide. Henceforth, the daily exchange rate of the Australian dollar was reported nightly on the news, just before the weather, like a barometric measure of Australia's international standing – which, in a way, it was. And in the mid-1980s, it was falling fast.

In 1983, the Australian dollar had floated at parity with the US dollar. But three years later it was around US$0.60. The main culprit was a fall in commodity prices. The message was clear: the structure of the economy that had underpinned Australia's relative prosperity for 150 years was no longer working and Australia was living beyond its means. In the nineteenth century we had the world's highest per capita income; now we were on the slide.

A sense of crisis gripped Australia's political elites, most memorably expressed in May 1986 by Treasurer Paul Keating. From a wall phone at the back of a restaurant, he told John Laws' Sydney morning radio program that we risked becoming a banana republic:

> We took the view in the 1970s – it's the old cargo cult mentality of Australia that she'll be right. This is the lucky country, we can dig up another mound of rock and someone will buy it from us, or we can sell a bit of wheat and bit of wool and we will just sort of muddle through … We are selling more coal and more iron ore and more of the agricultural products of late by volume than we have for years. But the prices and so the earnings are down …
>
> In the 1970s … we became a third-world economy selling raw materials and food and we let the sophisticated industrial side fall apart … If this government cannot get … manufacturing going again, and keep moderate wage outcomes and a sensible economic policy, then Australia is basically done for. We will just end up being a third-rate economy, a banana republic.

Get manufacturing going. Our resource exports, no matter how efficient, could not go on supporting our protected uncompetitive manufacturing; and wild fluctuation in commodity prices subjected the economy to periodic shocks over which the government had no control. But we were starting from a low base. In 1987, only 18 per cent of our exports were capital-intensive, elaborately transformed manufactures. For the United States, the figure was 68 per cent.

A key audience for Keating's banana republic outburst was the union movement. Labor had negotiated an accord with the ACTU to strengthen the social safety net, but many union members would be hurt by lower tariffs. Labor developed plans to restructure industries and started to dismantle the tariff wall. The aim was to diversify by developing internationally competitive export industries that could stand on their own two feet. Keating was placing his faith in getting the macroeconomic settings, such as the exchange, inflation and interest rates right, but the minister for industry, John Button, was sceptical that many firms could make the transition without support, and he did not think that sunrise industries would develop without government fostering links between education and business, and encouraging innovation.

Companies were not given much time. In 1988, the government announced that tariffs would be reduced to 10 or 15 per cent by 1992; and then in 1991, it announced a further reduction to a single rate of 5 per cent by 1996. Exceptions were made for the textile, clothing and footwear and car industries, which had their own plans. Both had high levels of protection, but they were big employers. And no one could yet imagine an advanced industrial economy without a car industry.

Just how far behind world's best practice Australian industry had fallen is illustrated by an anecdote of Button's. In 1987, Carlo Benetton, one of the founders of the Italian fashion house Benetton, wanted to invest in a weaving mill in Australia using our fine wool. He inspected two mills. One was quite modern, but too small for his needs. The other was antique. We have not had machines like that in Italy for sixty years, he told Button. "This is a young and beautiful country. How come you have such a terrible manufacturing plant? What is wrong with your business people?" There are many such anecdotes illustrating just how uncompetitive Australian manufacturing had become in the decades since the war. And there are detailed stories to be told about the various plans and policy adjustments to revive it. But the big story is that none of it worked.

When Bob Hawke died in May 2019, the media was full of praise for the way he and Keating had reformed Australia's financial system and internationalised its economy. Little was said, though, about the failure of the government's industry policy, that its attempt to develop exports of elaborately transformed manufactures to make Australia less dependent on exports from the farm and the quarry had come to nothing. This was Keating's main game as treasurer, and in 2019 it seemed all but forgotten.

In 1996, after thirteen years of Labor, the Coalition won government in a landslide. Its first Budget made significant cuts to Labor's programs to help industry innovate, including cuts to tax breaks for research and development. Howard, though, was more pragmatic than the neoliberal zealots in his party, and his government did maintain support for selected industries, most notably the car industry, which was becoming more internationally competitive. By 2007, it was one of Australia's top ten export earners, ahead of the agricultural exports of wool, wheat and wine.

Australia's export base also diversified during the 1990s with the growth of services. Cheap air travel fuelled international tourism which benefited Australia, and international secondary and tertiary students were starting to come here. By 1992, there were 50,000, up from just 5000 in 1986. Rapid improvements in information technology also enabled the export of specialised technical and professional services.

For a decade or so around the turn of the century, it seemed that Australian manufacturing might thrive. A 2007 Coalition-initiated inquiry concluded that it had a strong future:

> For the last two decades, Australian manufacturing has been making the transition from an inward-looking sector producing for a protected domestic market to an outward-looking sector competing in tough international markets. Despite large reductions in protection, the challenge from China and the high exchange rate associated with the resources boom, the Australian manufacturing sector as a whole has managed to survive and expand – albeit not at the rate of the overall economy.

The sector's share of exports was increasing – in fact, we had the fastest rate of increase in volumes of manufactured exports in the developed world – and it employed a respectable 21 per cent of the workforce, a figure similar to those of the United States, Canada and the UK.

But as a share of the economy, manufacturing was sliding, something the report fudged. Just under 12 per cent of GDP in 2000, by 2006 it was just over 10 per cent. And it has continued to slide. In 2018, it was 5.8 per cent, the same as mining, and its share of employment at 7.5 per cent was a third of 2007's respectable 21, though it was still a good deal more than mining's 1.9 per cent. What had happened?

*

The rise of China stopped the fragile revitalisation of our manufacturing in its tracks, but we scarcely noticed as the resources boom kicked off and made us rich again. In 2003, after a decade in the doldrums, commodity prices started to rise. Iron ore went rapidly from US$30 per ton to peak at almost US$200 per ton in 2008. Like many commodities, it is subject to big price swings, and the chart is up and down, but it has stayed well above US$30. This year it has fluctuated between a high of US$96.54 on the last day of January, just before the reality of COVID-19 sank in, and a low of US$80.54. Thermal coal also took off from 2003, from less than US$30 per ton to a peak of US$180 in 2008. It too is up and down, and at the end of 2019 was US$66 per ton. Massive improvement in our terms of trade followed, peaking in 2011 at the highest in 140 years.

Between 1991 and 2008, our economy expanded by just under 80 per cent. In 1995, our GDP per head put us in the bottom third of OECD countries; by 2008, we were back in the top third, where we believed we belonged. The gloom of the 1980s was a thing of the past and policy-makers were optimistic that China's demand for our resources would continue for the foreseeable future. So instead of thinking hard about the economy, the government was free to focus on attacking identity politics, fighting the history wars and distributing largesse to retirees and middle-class taxpayers.

The first hit to manufacturing came from the increasing value of the dollar, which rose with the price of commodities. In 2001, it was worth

US$0.49, and in 2004 US$0.79. This was not good for exporters. A low dollar helps them, making their goods and services cheaper on the global market and so more competitive. And it helps domestic producers by making imports more expensive. A high dollar has the reverse effects, making our exports expensive and our imports cheap.

The second hit was the phenomenal rise of Chinese manufacturing. From a relatively low base at the end of the twentieth century, by 2015 China accounted for 20 per cent of the world's manufacturing output and had surpassed the United States. By the mid-2000s, China was the major source of Australia's imports and it has stayed there. Even as the growth of Chinese steel production expanded the market for our iron ore, the expansion of its manufacturing of everything from clothes, shoes and household goods to computers and power tools drove companies worldwide out of business.

When Labor started to dismantle the protective tariff walls to expose Australian manufacturers to the bracing winds of global competition, it hoped that this would toughen them up. Instead, it blew most of them away. Companies still in business retained management and design functions in Australia but shifted their manufacturing to China. The price of manufactured imports fell rapidly. The few textile, clothing and footwear firms that had survived the reduction in tariffs could not survive competition with goods made in China. Clothes became ridiculously cheap, as did many other consumer goods. You can now buy a shirt or a dress from a discount department store for less than $10.

The sharp fall in the price of manufactured goods shifted their value relative to raw commodities. In the 1950s, we were having to produce more and more bags of wheat and bales of hay to pay for the same quantity of imported goods. This relationship now reversed.

Australia weathered the 2007–09 global financial crisis largely unscathed thanks in part to China's demand for our exports, but soon after that, manufacturing began another dramatic slide as a share of the economy and a source of jobs. As services grow in advanced economies, a relative decline in the contribution of manufacturing is to be expected, but this decline was absolute. Australian manufacturing was entering a death spiral.

The biggest casualty of Australia's mining boom was the car industry, struggling to build exports against a high dollar, which between 2011 and mid-2013 hovered around US$1. In 2013, there were three car manufacturers left in Australia: Ford, Toyota and General Motors Holden. Mid-year, Ford announced it would cease production at its Geelong and Broadmeadows factories within three years. Toyota and Holden were considering their future. The high dollar was increasing the cost of imported components and making it hard to expand exports. The Labor government was committed to maintaining an Australian car industry and the industry minister, Kim Carr, was in negotiations with Holden about government support for its plan to build the next generation of Commodores and Cruzes in Australia. The Victorian and South Australian governments were coming on board with some assistance. Kevin Rudd, who had just been re-elected Labor's leader in an effort to save some furniture in the upcoming election, said, "I never want to be prime minister of a country that doesn't make things anymore."

Carr's negotiations with Holden were overtaken by the election at the beginning of September 2013, which Labor lost. The new government, with Tony Abbott as prime minister and Joe Hockey as treasurer, did not feel the same commitment to an Australian car industry, which was centred in the Labor-leaning states of Victoria and South Australia. The Coalition's impatience with the industry's dependence on government subsidy was clear. Holden would not say how much assistance was requested, but reports from the time suggest Holden needed an additional payment of between $150 million and $265 million to build the two new models in Australia.

Early in December, Prime Minister Abbott said that there would be no money over and above the generous support already available, and a few days later, in parliamentary Question Time, Joe Hockey let fly at Holden over its reluctance to make its long-term intentions clear, demanding that

Holden "come clean" over its future in the country. "Either you're here or you're not," he said. When management in head office in Detroit heard this, they decided they were not. Toyota wanted to stay. It had a business plan and an export market, but without Holden it was not viable, as there would not be enough business to support a healthy network of local suppliers. So it too decided to go, and within a few years Australia no longer had a car industry. Ironically, soon after, the dollar started to fall. By 2015, it was around US$0.70, a much more competitive value for exporters, but by then it was too late. The decisions had been made.

Is this what Hockey intended as he engaged in the usual rough and tumble of Question Time? It certainly fitted with the neoliberal political agenda of removing impediments to the operations of the market so that nations can pursue their areas of comparative advantage unencumbered. But for many it marked the end of Australia's long-held aspiration to be a modern industrial nation. We are no longer a country that makes much. We do still make some things, chiefly things that can't be moved about – buildings, fences, roads and other infrastructure – but our industrial capacity has been severely compromised.

Hockey and Abbott's cavalier attitude to the Australian car industry was evidence of the lack of depth in too many of our political leaders' understanding of economics. They can read a balance sheet, but fail to understand the real world that produced it. The car industry is central to a country's industrial development. It is capital- and knowledge-intensive, depends on a large range of highly developed skills, and stimulates scientific and technological progress in other complex manufacturing industries. Advanced industrial economies such as Germany and the United States subsidise their car industries because it helps sustain advanced manufacturing.

Media coverage of the demise of the Australian car industry highlighted the lost jobs, the personal cost to workers and the uncertain future they faced. Many have since found work, and others have retired. When, earlier this year, General Motors announced it would also stop importing and selling the Holden brand, there was an outpouring of nostalgia for

Holdens past. But the country has lost much more than tens of thousands of stable, well-paid jobs and a cultural icon. It has lost capacity, and this has serious consequences, especially for those who worry about whether we could defend ourselves in the event of a war.

In February this year, the French company that won the contract to build the Collins submarine in Adelaide reported that it was having difficulty meeting its contract requirement to source 50 per cent of its production from Australian suppliers. The CEO of the project, John Davis, said that a key issue was the prevalence of small and medium-sized firms in the defence sector. Although highly innovative, they did not have the capability to meet the project's needs. In response, the Department of Defence released a list of 137 subcontractors to show that local firms were benefiting, but it included just six defence equipment suppliers and twenty-eight engineering firms. The rest were firms supplying services such as accounting, travel and recruitment. Even Alliance Française was on the list, so that local staff could brush up on their French. All these contribute to local employment, but they do not build a skilled defence workforce. To repeat a statistic given earlier, at the end of 2019 we had fewer than 100,000 skilled metal workers. The fragile recovery of our manufacturing at the turn of the century could not survive the rise of China, nor Hockey and Abbott's reckless abandonment of the car industry.

The COVID-19 pandemic has made Australians painfully aware of just how little we now make here. When it hit, we had one small factory in rural Victoria making surgical masks, and none making the ventilators needed to treat people seriously ill from coronavirus. Since then, the mask-making factory has ramped up production with help from the defence forces, a consortium of manufacturing and engineering firms has been formed to produce 2000 ventilators, and some companies have pivoted their operations to making sanitisers and protective screens. The current minister for industry, science and technology, Karen Andrews, says this is a reflection of "the highly advanced manufacturing capability that exists in our country." It would be comforting to think so, but whatever potential there is, our manufacturing sector is today only a remnant of what we once had. A trained engineer, Andrews is the most visible industry minister we have had for some time, and appears to be genuinely committed to rebuilding Australia's manufacturing capacity. At present, everyone agrees we need to be able to make personal protective equipment for medical staff, and perhaps some medical equipment and medicines. But what else?

Morrison has indicated that the government is considering how to safeguard Australia's "domestic economic sovereignty," but he also says this needs to be balanced against our history as "an open trading nation." The Liberal Party has just reversed decades of its thinking about government-provided income support. Will it also be able to modify its belief in the overriding virtues of free trade and its reluctance to provide targeted industry support? Even if Morrison is persuaded, supported by conservative colleagues concerned about defence and national security, he will face strong opposition from fellow Liberals raised on the belief that anything smacking of protection or of governments "picking winners" is anathema. And then the government will need to cooperate with the states to rebuild the shattered TAFE system so that it can train people to work in a rejuvenated manufacturing sector.

*

The first half of this essay has been about the way Australia's dependence on trade in primary commodities has shaped our economy, disconnecting exports from employment in the cities where most of us live, and contributing to our failure to build a resilient manufacturing sector. Were it not for the climate crisis, the story could end here. The impact of the resource curse would be relatively benign, a story about sectoral competition and the consequence of Australia pursuing its comparative advantage in natural resources. There would still be concerns about our self-sufficiency if global supply chains were seriously disrupted, but mining's social licence would be unaffected. This is not, however, the world we live in. Levels of carbon dioxide in the atmosphere have been rising since the Industrial Revolution began burning coal. They are now rising fast, with a discernible effect on global temperatures. The vast majority of the world's scientists have told us that to reduce the severity of catastrophic changes to the climate we need to stop burning fossil fuels. Unsurprisingly, fossil-fuel miners have fought back hard. The second part of this essay looks at the political face of the resource curse, beginning with the miners' successful campaigns against Indigenous rights.

Australians were generally happy to ride on the sheep's back. Many of us are not at all happy to be riding in a coal cart. Australia has robust legal institutions and our politics is relatively democratic and accountable, but since the turn of the century fossil-fuel miners have massively increased their influence over both sides of politics, and over state and federal governments. The main game has been to head off government action to reduce carbon emissions. This has weakened Australia's willingness to play its part in reducing global warming, but the effects of the curse have spread beyond this, contributing to debilitating political polarisation.

The first Australians to suffer from the politics of the resource curse were Indigenous Australians. During the 1980s and 1990s, as the mining lobby effectively weakened legislation on land rights and native title, it developed the strategies it would later use to stymie effective government action on climate change.

When the Australian Mining Industries Council (AMIC) was formed in 1967, its initial aims were conventional industry matters, such as the rules governing foreign investment or the exchange rate. But mining was starting to face a quite different set of challenges. The new mining boom was concentrated in Australia's north, where many Indigenous Australians had continued to live on or close to their country. Some groups were demanding land rights, including the capacity to veto mining. As well, conservationists were pushing the government on mining's environmental impact, and there was suspicion of the extent of foreign ownership. Because mining employed few people, it could rely less on electoral pressure than other economic interest groups. The miners needed to convince the public that mining was crucial to national development and prosperity and so should not be curtailed.

In 1972, AMIC imposed a special levy on its members to fund campaigns focused on mass audiences rather than governments. Contacts in the media were fostered; articles and advertisements placed in newspapers,

TV and radio; material prepared for public affairs programs. There was even consideration given to producing literature for schools, "so that school children will grow up with a sound knowledge and understanding of the mining industry and the benefits it is providing for their future."

In 1973, the new Labor government's minister for minerals and energy, Rex Connor, commissioned a report on the contribution of mining to Australia's welfare. The report by economist Tom Fitzgerald questioned the assumption that mining was inherently beneficial to the Australian economy and confirmed the industry's conviction that it could not take the public's support for granted.

Western Mining's Hugh Morgan, who in 1976 would become the company's executive director, identified the report as a turning point both for himself and the industry. He realised, he later told Gerard Henderson, that to survive, the mining industry had to persuade the community of its benefits and take on its adversaries. Ray Evans, a conservative engineer, was hired as a speechwriter to assist with these tasks.

By the early 1980s, Morgan and Evans were leading figures in what was then called the Australian New Right, a loose network of conservative men – and a few women – in high places, who combined a zeal for free-market economics with opposition to the progressive causes of the 1970s, including land rights and environmentalism. Through think-tanks such as the Institute of Public Affairs and the Centre for Independent Studies, through newsletters and conferences, private dinners and informal gatherings, they developed arguments and strategies to counter what they saw as a dangerous left-wing grip on public opinion. "Politicians can only accept what is accepted in the public opinion polls, so you have to change public opinion," Morgan told Paul Sheehan of *The Sydney Morning Herald* in 1985. By then, he had become a vehement opponent of Indigenous land rights.

Gough Whitlam had taken a commitment to land rights to the 1972 election. In government, he appointed Justice Edward Woodward to conduct a royal commission into Aboriginal land rights in the Northern Territory. Woodward's recommendations were revolutionary. Here are some: all Aboriginal reserve lands were to be returned to their Aboriginal inhabitants; Aboriginal people could claim vacant Crown land on the basis of traditional ties with the land; and most important for the subject of this essay, entry into Aboriginal land for mining and tourism required the consent of the local community. Aboriginal people were to be given the possibility of vetoing mining developments, and mining companies would have to pay royalties to the traditional owners, though the Commonwealth retained the power to overrule any Aboriginal veto in the national interest. If adopted, Justice Woodward's recommendations would dramatically reset the balance of power between mining companies and Indigenous Australians and they would give Indigenous landholders rights to control mining which were not available to non-Indigenous freehold owners.

After the Whitlam government was dismissed at the end of 1975, the incoming Liberal prime minister, Malcolm Fraser, generally supported Woodward's recommendations, and his government passed the *Aboriginal Land Rights (Northern Territory) Act* in 1976. Pastoralists, miners and many Coalition members thought Fraser had conceded far too much to Indigenous interests. AMIC wanted the veto abolished and royalties reduced, as did the Northern Territory government, which saw the Act as a brake on development.

By the early 1980s, a patchwork of laws and practices governed land rights across the continent. Labor took a commitment to uniform land-rights legislation to the 1983 election, promising to use Commonwealth powers to override uncooperative states. The draft proposed minimum uniform land rights across the states and territories, including protection of sacred sites, a veto over mining, and royalties. Conservatives of all stripes were alarmed and a fear campaign began, led by AMIC and the Western Australian Chamber of Mines, with media releases, opinion pieces, and press, radio and TV advertising, including full-page advertisements in national newspapers.

The public campaign was designed to make ordinary Australians with no direct involvement in mining feel they had a stake in disputes happening far from where they lived. The centrepiece was the argument that Aborigines should not have special rights. AMIC distributed speakers' notes with arguments such as: "Land rights should be equal rights, not greater rights"; "Australia is one country and there should be one set of laws for everyone"; "No country can be divided against itself and survive." It claimed that the proposed legislation had the power to lock up a quarter of Australia's surface, bring mining exploration to a halt and damage the nation's prosperity. In Western Australia, a TV ad showed a black hand reaching across the state to build a wall: the message was that land rights would lock up vast areas of territory.

The appeal to equality rejected arguments that Aboriginal people's distinctive relationship to the land, and their distinctive suffering as a colonised people, entitled them to special rights or treatment. It was a powerful appeal and support for land rights started to fall, among both the public and elected politicians. The Western Australian premier, Brian Burke, told Hawke that the commitment to uniform land rights could cost Labor up to eight seats in Western Australia at the 1984 federal election. Hawke dropped the veto over mining exploration, and by 1986 the government had effectively abandoned the promise of uniform legislation, leaving the states to do as they wished. Although Aboriginal people in the Northern Territory still had the right to negotiate over mines and royalties, the campaign had succeeded in preventing this arrangement spreading to other states, and AMIC had protected its members' interests. Then came the High Court's 1992 Mabo judgment, when the miners needed to defend themselves all over again.

Land rights were legislated rights, created by the state and federal parliaments, and they did not challenge European Australia's foundational assumption that when Captain Cook claimed Australia for the Crown there were no pre-existing property rights, that it was *terra nullius*. The High Court's finding that in certain circumstances a form of native title might still exist unleashed an even nastier and more divisive campaign than the one waged against uniform land rights. Rural and mining investment would be discouraged and the economy damaged, it was claimed.

Hugh Morgan called on the Coalition to overrule the Mabo decision if they won government by passing legislation to extinguish native title. As this would open the government to unknown claims for compensation for the extinguished rights, conservatives also called for the 1975 *Racial Discrimination Act* to be overturned so that native title rights could be abolished without compensation. Victorian premier Jeff Kennett played on fears by falsely suggesting that even suburban backyards could be at risk.

Paul Keating, who was now prime minister, saw the Mabo judgment as a historic judgment that laid the foundation for reconciliation. Others saw it very differently. State governments did not want to concede their rights over land titles; mining and pastoral interests were alarmed about the potential impact on their leases; and many, but not all, of the Coalition opposed Aborigines being treated any differently from other Australians. After extensive consultations, including with Indigenous groups, the *Native Title Act* passed at the end of 1993. Native title holders could negotiate over development, but they did not hold any veto powers.

The Mabo judgment was clear that freehold title extinguished native title, but it said nothing about leases. At the end of 1996 another High Court judgment in a case bought by the Wik people of Aurukun found that leases did not necessarily extinguish native title. The judgment ushered in another round of bitter conflict over Indigenous rights and another round of dire predictions about the impact on mining investment. The new prime minister, John Howard, held up to the television camera a map of Australia showing just how much of the continent might be subject to claims. The National Party's leader, Tim Fischer, toured the bush calling for "bucket-loads of extinguishment," as if native title was a fire threat. Howard rejected extinguishment because of the unknown compensation it would trigger, but the ten-point plan he developed severely curtailed the rights of native title holders and did not include the right to negotiate with mining companies on pastoral leases.

The campaigns against uniform land rights and then native title built an alliance between the National Party and Australia's miners. Miners could spruik their contribution to Australia's national prosperity, but they were hard-pressed to give this a human face. The National Party could provide any number: weathered old farmers talking about their pioneering forebears and their deep love of the land; or young couples living in the outback and raising their kids far from city amenities. These tough men and women wearing Akubras and standing in outback landscapes were invaluable to the miners' campaign to associate the fight against native title with a shared national heritage, to make it seem relevant to the vast majority of Australians, who would never be affected by a native title claim.

The campaign was also invaluable to the National Party. Beginning life in 1920 as the Australian Country Party to represent farmers and rural communities, its base was shrinking. There were fewer farming families and small rural service towns were dying. In 1975, it changed its name to the National Country Party, and in 1982 to the National Party of Australia to try to broaden its base from conservative country folk to like-minded outer-suburban voters. It didn't really work, and the decline continued. When Fraser defeated Whitlam at the end of 1975, the National Country Party won 11.04 per cent of the national first preference vote and twenty-two seats. In 1996, when Howard defeated Keating, it was 8.2 per cent and eighteen seats.

The problems facing the National Party were not just a shrinking base but uncertainty about what it stood for. Its Coalition partner was enthusiastically embracing free-market policies, which threatened the many subsidised services country people enjoyed. Yet it could not openly break with the Liberals and risk its cabinet positions. Fighting against Aboriginal land rights gave it new relevance, and the miners paid for advertisements which reminded the public that the Australians at the heart of the country were the men and women on the land.

The fight over the Mabo and Wik legislation consolidated conservative opposition to Indigenous rights, to policies of positive discrimination for Indigenous Australians, and to historians who highlighted the violence and injustices of the European invasion rather than the achievements of settlement and material progress. To the long-term detriment of Indigenous people, it also consolidated their identification with Labor in the minds of Coalition politicians and supporters. The bipartisanship apparent at the end of the 1970s had gone. After John Howard won the 1996 federal election, policies seen to favour Indigenous Australians were an immediate target, frequently justified with one-line arguments about equality straight from AMIC's 1980s speakers' notes against land rights. The miners were defending their economic interests but in doing this they had weakened public sympathy for Aboriginal people and popularised arguments against their distinctive rights. Here was the resource curse in action. Pauline Hanson rode into parliament on such arguments, and they are trotted out regularly by conservatives.

The big miners did subsequently work hard to repair their credentials with Indigenous Australians, developing strategies to boost employment, offering scholarships and cadetships, employing archaeologists and anthropologists to advise on cultural heritage. BHP, Rio Tinto, Glencore and Fortescue all proclaim a commitment to engaging with Indigenous people and outline various targeted programs on their websites. They could be generous once they had won.

The mining industry's campaign against land rights and native title gave it the capacity to mount public relations and advertising campaigns to defend its interests and the confidence that it could win; and it created a network of influential right-wing warriors primed to defend Australia's existing distribution of power and resources. When climate change began seriously to threaten fossil-fuel miners at the end of last century, they knew what to do. To prevent the development of bipartisan consensus on climate action, they needed to position scepticism about climate change firmly on the same side of the political divide as opposition to Indigenous rights.

During the 1990s, a global coal rush was getting underway, as China, India and Japan all built new power stations, creating surging demand for Australian coal. At the same time, climate scientists were insisting that the burning of fossil fuels needed to be urgently and drastically reduced to combat global warming, some policy-makers were considering ways to price carbon, and a public climate movement was growing. Fossil-fuel producers needed a united position to ward off government moves that would curtail their growth. They especially wanted to prevent the federal government from signing international agreements committing to reducing carbon emissions. As in the campaigns against land rights and native title, the aim was to align the interests of miners with the national interest. Their core argument was that mining underpinned Australia's wealth, so policies that reduced carbon emissions would damage the whole economy.

After Howard won the 1996 election, it became much easier for the mining lobby to prevent action on climate change. Australia negotiated a special deal for itself at the 1997 Kyoto climate conference on the basis of our geographical location and size and our dependence on fossil fuels a deal which the government then refused to ratify. The Howard government did legislate to require large energy providers to use a very small amount of renewable energy in order to encourage investment. The original renewable energy target (RET) of 2 per cent was modest, but for many fossil-fuel advocates it was still a step too far.

Guy Pearse, who worked for environment minister Robert Hill, had a ringside seat as the mining lobby hammered environmentalists and undermined Hill's tentative efforts to develop policies to limit Australia's emissions. The Australian Industry Greenhouse Network (AIGN) was formed as an umbrella group within the Minerals Council of Australia (the new name for AMIC). Key players called themselves "the greenhouse mafia" and sometimes "the mob." These names, Pearse wrote, accurately captured their disproportionate behind-the-scenes influence.

Pearse subsequently did a PhD at the Australian National University on the power of the carbon lobby in the Howard government. He interviewed more than fifty insiders, who, under the cloak of anonymity, were keen to boast of their power. His research was the basis for a 2006 ABC *Four Corners* program on "The Greenhouse Mafia," as well as for his book *High and Dry: John Howard, climate change and the selling of Australia's future*. Pearse revealed the intimate relationships between key lobbyists and senior bureaucrats in the relevant departments, as the lobbyists gained access to confidential reports and were given privileged input to the formation of policy on climate change, including on occasion writing cabinet submissions.

Most were recruited from the senior bureaucracy and ministers' offices, creating a round robin of advice among people who already knew and trusted each other and making the greenhouse mafia an extraordinarily powerful lobbying alliance. As one boasted to Pearse, "We all write the same way, we all think the same way, we all worked for the same set of ministers." Similar access was not given to environmental NGOs.

An industry advancing its interests through lobbying, public advocacy and political donations is perfectly legal in Australia, and to be expected in an open pluralist society where governments have to develop policies that take account of a range of competing interests. What Pearse documents is much more than this. It is state capture, in which a private interest is able to shape government's decisions to its own advantage. This is the political face of the resource curse.

Telling evidence is the lack of access to government policy-making given to environmental and community groups which oppose the expansion of mining. In making climate policy, the Australian federal government has not listened to the arguments of all interested groups as if it were a neutral umpire, because it was already captured by advocates of fossil fuels. To be sure, the mining industry had powerful arguments to make about its contribution to the Australian economy, but so did the environmentalists and climate scientists about the dangers of rising global temperatures. A prudent government concerned with the national interest and Australia's long-term security would have listened to them too, rather than excluding them from the process. Politicians talk often about the need to balance the competing goods of economic and environmental outcomes, but this assumes that voices speaking for environmental outcomes are part of the process.

That they weren't is because, under Howard, climate denial and scepticism spread through the Australian right. If you believe that climate change is not a problem, then you won't see any need to include environmentalists and climate scientists in policy formation. Australia did not invent climate denialism, of course – it was imported from the United States. But it has been more influential here than almost anywhere else.

In March 2000, the dynamic duo of Western Mining's Hugh Morgan and Ray Evans turned their skills in networking and agitation to the formation of the Lavoisier Group to combat action on climate change. Named after the French chemist Antoine-Laurent de Lavoisier, the group's aims were to challenge the science on global warming, to persuade the Australian government not to sign binding international agreements to reduce emissions, and to defeat measures such as a carbon tax. Its website records that the founders:

> were deeply concerned at the drift in policy development that was then apparent at the highest levels of the Canberra mandarinate. Decarbonisation of the economy was inevitable, it was being said, and the sooner we all had to adjust to carbon taxes the better.
>
> It was not obvious to us that, first, decarbonisation was inevitable and, second, that the science on which these conclusions were based was beyond reproach.

Morgan and Evans had long been suspicious of environmentalism as a new form of revolutionary anti-capitalism. In 1989, as the Cold War was ending, Morgan wrote an article in *Quadrant* warning that environmentalists were the new communists: "The Environmentalists are unrelenting in their attack on private property, constantly asserting that property rights must be subject, more and more, to political discretion, in order to preserve and save the environment." As environmentally aware scientists started to warn of the dangers of climate change, Morgan and Evans didn't miss a beat. Said Evans, it took him "about five minutes to realise that the whole thing was a scam," that the assessments of the Intergovernmental Panel on Climate Change were based on junk science; and that the CSIRO, the Bureau of Meteorology and Malcolm Turnbull were all swallowing complete bullshit. Where the industry lobby focused on economic arguments, the Lavoisier Group's aim was to build a cohort of climate sceptics and deniers within Australia's political and business elites, through conferences and seminars, and through its website, which linked members into a global network of climate science deniers.

The Lavoisier Group's immediate objective was to persuade the Howard government not to ratify the Kyoto Protocol. This was the first of the legally binding international agreements to reduce global emissions, and opposition to it drew not just on rejection of the protocol's purpose, but on the right's suspicion of international agreements that went beyond the traditional diplomatic concerns of war, peace and trade. This suspicion dated from the early years of the Hawke government, when it used the external affairs power to prevent the Tasmanian government from damming the Franklin River to expand its hydro-electric scheme.

The Lavoisier Group's founding board was dominated by men from mining and energy companies, except for a star recruit from the left, ex–Western Australian Labor senator Peter Walsh, who was the first president. Walsh had been a minister in the Hawke governments, first for energy and resources in 1983 to '84, and then for finance from 1984 to 1990. He was openly hostile to environmentalism, which he believed was taking the Labor Party away from its blue-collar working-class roots in order "to appease bourgeois Left and middle-class trendoids in the gentrified suburbs of Sydney and Melbourne."

The Lavoisier Group was not the only influential Australian agent of climate denial. The Institute of Public Affairs had been busy attacking evidence-based climate science since the late 1980s. To the IPA, climate change was not a matter of fact, but of belief or opinion. Those who disputed this were then accused of dogmatism and attacks on free speech, thus linking climate scepticism to a core Liberal belief. At the extreme end of this argument was the claim that belief in climate change was a new religion.

The Murdoch press, together with Sky News, also fostered doubts about the facts of global warming and the effectiveness of anything Australia might do, even if it turned out to be true. Robert Manne analysed articles and opinion pieces on climate change in Murdoch's *Australian* between January 2004 and April 2011, when it was edited by Chris Mitchell. Out of 880 articles, Manne classified 700 as unfavourable to climate change action. Many of the unfavourable articles were written by people with no qualifications at all in any relevant discipline, but with "a comical degree of self-confidence" in their ill-informed opinions and contempt for their opponents, whom they regularly mocked and denigrated. The anti–climate change agenda could also always rely on radio shock-jocks Alan Jones and Ray Hadley, or on Melbourne's Andrew Bolt, to attack and mock anyone arguing for action on climate change, whether they be climate scientists or environmental activists.

Howard won the 1996 election in part by sharpening up the lines of grievance that had been forming since the recession at the end of the 1980s. Labor's neoliberal reform agenda was elite-driven, with low levels of public support and understanding. Many blue-collar workers employed in manufacturing or by the large state-owned utilities lost their jobs, as did the mainly female workforce in the textile, clothing and footwear factories. People were generally suspicious of privatisation, and country dwellers feared for their cross-subsidised services. The Coalition supported these economic changes, but it was less enthusiastic about Labor's social and cultural policies, such as affirmative action for women, and environmentalism. Some members were also arguing for a return to a traditional Australian nationalism, in contrast to Labor's vision of Australia as a multicultural nation drawing closer to Asia, and as we have seen, the Coalition was firmly against any "special treatment" of Indigenous Australians.

Under Howard, the Coalition constructed a binary political world. On one side were supporters of affirmative action for women, multiculturalism, racial inclusiveness, native title, Indigenous self-determination and reconciliation; acknowledgment of the violence and injustice towards Indigenous people; greater environmental regulation; an Australian republic; a commitment to internationalism. All of this was identified with Labor and the Greens. On the other side were people who regarded affirmative action for women and Indigenous Australians as unfair, supported assimilation for Indigenous Australians, rejected "black armband" history, opposed too much environmental regulation, thought people had a right to be bigots, and supported traditional Australian nationalism.

The overlaps were imprecise, but it was a powerful set of binary pairs. Opposition to action on climate change was firmly situated on the conservative side of this partisan divide, and the possibility of bipartisan action was destroyed for at least two decades. That some of these oppositions clearly were differences of value and belief reinforced the argument that climate change too was a matter of value and belief. For the right, the culture wars morphed smoothly into the climate wars. Some senior ministers and backbenchers, as well as senior party officials and fundraisers, were avowed deniers. One senior Lavoisier figure boasted to Pearse that "there was an understanding in the cabinet that the science is all crap."

Under Howard, climate scepticism if not outright denial became a key identifier of the Australian right. Climate denial has its strongest grip on aging white men, drawing on their need for certainty and control, the aggressive self-confidence they mobilise to defend these, and the projection of their own threatened sense of identity onto others. One of the more ridiculous accusations climate deniers make against climate activists is that it is an identity issue and that worrying about the climate is virtue-signalling. In fact, it is just the opposite.

Last year, I was invited to address a session of the annual conference of the Samuel Griffith Society on Alfred Deakin and federalism. Twice during my brief time there, another attendee made unprompted dismissive comments about people who believed in climate change. A mild-mannered elderly woman told me it was a religion, a blustery elderly man that it was a Marxist conspiracy. Were they testing my conservative credentials, I wondered, or did they just expect everyone they met to be a climate change sceptic?

Two Swedish social scientists who conducted a focus group with climate sceptics concluded that for these people, "it was not the environment that was threatened, it was a certain kind of modern industrial society built and dominated by their form of masculinity." The focus group participants, with one exception, were aging white men who had held prominent positions in academia and large companies. The researchers concluded that their climate scepticism was linked to their fears about the disappearance of the masculine-dominated industrial modernity in which they had enjoyed power and success. Subsequent research by the same group has found a complementary identification of science and concern for the environment with the feminine. Nature as feminine to the masculinity of control over it is a well-established structure in Western thought, so these findings are not surprising. But they are disturbing. When a political opinion is embedded in the core of a person's identity, it is hard to reach with evidence and arguments, no matter how compelling. It is also resistant to the bargaining and compromise that successful political outcomes depend on. Soon after Angus Taylor became energy minister in Morrison's government, he told an *AFR* Energy Summit, "There is no room for bipartisanship when we have a 26 per cent [reduction target] and the other side has 45 per cent." Maybe, but there is room for compromise. The two sides could meet halfway, as unions and employers do regularly when bargaining on conditions and wages.

After Howard lost office, and particularly since Abbott's tenure as prime minister, a succession of aging politicians have publicly espoused their climate scepticism – Craig Kelly, Malcolm Roberts and Jim Molan, to name the most memorable. Kelly is a fool and Roberts a stubborn contrarian, but Molan is neither. He was a competent senior Australian military officer in various positions of command, who was required to make evidence-based judgments in matters of life and death. Yet on *Q&A* in February 2020, on a panel with climate scientist Michael Mann, he said that his mind was open on whether the climate change we were experiencing was human-induced. Mann replied, "You should keep an open mind, but not so open that your brains fall out." But for Molan, his views on climate change are not primarily about brains and evidence but a signal to fellow members of the Liberal Party's right that he is one of them.

With Howard as prime minister, the miners could be confident of policies favourable to fossil fuels. But public opinion was shifting. During 2007, Howard changed his public position on climate change and took an emissions trading scheme to the election at the end of the year. Explaining his apparent conversion, Howard later said that his government had run into "a perfect storm." The millennium drought was devastating farming and threatening city water supplies, the bushfire season had started early, and Al Gore's documentary *An Inconvenient Truth*, together with Gore's visits to Australia, had raised public awareness. A Lowy Institute opinion poll conducted in mid-2007 found climate change topping respondents' list of external threats to Australia.

In 2013, in a lecture to London's Orwellian-named Global Warming Policy Foundation, Howard admitted that his emissions trading scheme was not evidence of a changed mind, but a pragmatic political response to a shift in the public mood. At heart, he had stayed a sceptic.

Labor won the election in November 2007 in a landslide under its new leader, Kevin Rudd, who famously described climate change as "the great moral challenge of our generation." The fossil-fuel lobby adapted quickly to the new government, shifting its focus from business and profits to unions and jobs. Labor was less receptive to climate scepticism than the Coalition had been, but it was sensitive to predictions of massive job losses, especially in the coal industry. The Australian Workers' Union and the Construction, Forestry, Maritime, Mining and Energy Union, many of whose members worked for mining and energy companies, were immediate allies, and Peter Walsh – Walshie to his mates – was an invaluable door-opener. The new government was bombarded with arguments about the centrality of fossil fuels to the economy and the dire consequences of limiting emissions too much or too soon.

The centrepiece of the Rudd government's climate policies, unveiled in 2009, was an ETS, which would use market mechanisms to drive down emissions by putting a price on carbon. Coal was especially threatened. The Australian Coal Association, with the help of the Liberal Party's favourite PR firm Crosby Textor, ran a campaign focused on potential job losses. The slogan was "Let's cut emissions not jobs." In one newspaper advertisement a glum middle-aged man in a hi-vis shirt says, "The new tax on coal mines won't help climate change. So why should I lose my job for it?"

The campaign also convinced Coalition parliamentarians, among whom was a core of sceptics and deniers, to move against Liberal leader Malcolm Turnbull, who had negotiated an ETS with Rudd that the Coalition would support. Turnbull lost the leadership by one vote to Abbott, who opposed the ETS in any form. Labor's legislation now depended on the Greens, who regarded it as so compromised, with such generous compensation for the large carbon polluters, that they voted against it, and Rudd backed off. The ETS was dead.

In May 2010, the miners faced another challenge: the proposal for a tax on the super-profits they were making from the resources boom. The tax would garner more of these for the nation, but it was not only a revenue-raising measure. It was also part of a package of measures designed as a remedy for the Dutch disease Australia had caught as the resources boom pushed up the dollar to the detriment of non-mining exporters and drained labour and investment from other sectors. Australia was becoming a two-speed economy, with Queensland and Western Australia growing much faster than the other states. The idea was to replace royalties on the volumes of minerals produced with a tax on profits when they were sold, so that governments could get some benefit from the high commodity prices that were pushing up the dollar and killing manufacturing and tourism.

Treasurer Wayne Swan announced the tax in May 2010 and the big multinational miners swung into action, with BHP Billiton, Rio Tinto and Xstrata leading the charge. A war room was established inside BHP's head office in Melbourne. Focus groups were used to drive $22 million of advertising on TV and print media with the familiar warnings that the tax would cost jobs and drive away investment. There was a new claim, too, that the industry had protected Australia from the worst impacts of the global financial crisis. The same messages were conveyed in a lobbying campaign targeted at state and federal politicians.

The campaign was short, brutal and spectacularly successful. A little over seven weeks after the announcement of the tax, Rudd's approval ratings slumped. Acting from a combination of panic and hubris, Labor's parliamentary party deposed him as prime minister and installed Julia Gillard. This is likely more than the miners were aiming for. Rudd and Swan had sprung the tax without the stakeholder consultations expected in major reforms. Martin Ferguson, the federal minister for resources and energy and the government's main link with the industry, had been largely excluded from the process. All this consolidated mounting doubts about Rudd's erratic and autocratic leadership style. Even so, it was a formidable display of corporate power. In the two years since Rudd had been elected, the mining industry had derailed two of his major policies.

Gillard immediately negotiated a deal with the three big multinational miners for a minerals resource rent tax, which benefited them at the expense of smaller miners. It was a poorly designed, hobbled tax which ended up raising little revenue. Gillard sold the new tax as moving things forward, "whether you're a coalminer in the Bowen Basin, a contractor in Karratha, an opal miner in Cooper Pedy, or a young worker in Sydney." Just how the young Sydney worker was helped was not clear, except in a general narrative that mining underpinned our national prosperity – claiming to provide jobs was becoming the industry's core public defence. Journalist Paul Cleary wrote in 2011, "This episode highlights the growing power and influence of mining and energy companies. Increasingly these companies control our economy and environment in ways we have scarcely begun to comprehend."

However, the mining lobby was not able to stop Labor implementing a price on carbon, strengthening the renewable energy target, and establishing agencies such as the Australian Renewable Energy Agency (ARENA), the Clean Energy Finance Corporation (CEFC) and the Climate Change

Authority (CCA). According to Ross Garnaut, for two years from 1 July 2012 Australia had an efficient, effective and equitable set of emissions reductions policies largely governed by market principles. Emissions started to come down, and had they been left in place we would be well on the way to achieving net zero emissions by 2050.

Abbott had vowed to fight the mining resources tax "as long as there is breath in my political body," and he brought the same fanatical partisan energy to fighting the Gillard government's reworking of the ETS into a price on carbon, which he immediately labelled a "tax." He promised that if the Coalition won the next election there would be no mining tax and no carbon tax.

Under Abbott, the two decades of cultivation of a network of climate sceptics and deniers by the Lavoisier Group and the IPA paid off in spades. Abbott was openly and repeatedly sceptical about the science of climate change and, with his imprimatur, a hard core of climate sceptics formed inside the Coalition determined to stymie any policies aimed at reducing Australia's carbon emissions. In 2013, the threat of a carbon tax was used to defeat the Gillard government. Abbott's then chief of staff, Peta Credlin, later boasted about how easily she and Abbott had been able to bamboozle the public over Labor's carbon price.

> Along comes a carbon tax. It wasn't a carbon tax, as you know. It was many other things in nomenclature terms, but we made it a carbon tax. We made it a fight about the hip pocket and not about the environment. That was brutal retail politics and it took Abbott about six months to cut through and when he cut through, Gillard was gone.

So too, for the immediate future, was the possibility that Australia could develop bipartisan policies to reduce emissions. Some of Labor's initiatives survived the carnage, namely ARENA, the CEFC and the CCA, saved by the quixotic Clive Palmer, whose United Australia Party held the balance of power in the Senate. The party supported the repeal of the carbon price, but not the abolition of these agencies, nor of the RET. After meeting with Al Gore, Palmer said he had changed his mind about the science.

Under Abbott, denial and scepticism about climate science spread to science generally. It is scientists who have uncovered the evidence of global warming, explained it as a result of the carbon released into the atmosphere by the burning of fossil fuels since the Industrial Revolution, and warned of its potential catastrophic consequences. Abbott made his feelings clear by failing to include a minister for science in his first government. As well, his and Treasurer Joe Hockey's first Budget slashed funding to major scientific organisations such as Geoscience Australia and the CSIRO. In the way of things, as decision-makers sniff the wind, CSIRO management decided that much of the climate change–related research could be dispensed with.

The denigration of science has not only affected climate science. It has undermined the nation's commitment to research and development more broadly and fostered a silly hostility to new renewable energy technologies. Remember Hockey complaining about the ugly wind turbines on the road from Sydney to Canberra? Since 2013, when the Coalition came to power, funding for research and development in Australia as a percentage of GDP has declined by around 14 per cent. In 2017–18, it was 1.79 per cent, well below the OECD average of 2.37 per cent.

If we look only at federal government spending on R&D, removing state government and private sector contributions, the picture is even worse. In 2015, the federal government spent just 0.4 per cent on R&D, putting us down at the bottom of the pack, between Greece and Slovakia, just as we are low down on the Harvard index of the complexity and diversity of our exports. There is a link. Research and development seeds innovation, developing new sources of growth in the economy, in manufacturing, in services and in agriculture. The mining industry is not solely to blame for the anti-science philistinism that gripped the Coalition government under Abbott, but it does carry some responsibility for its self-interested casting of doubt on the findings of climate scientists.

Proof of just how comprehensively the Coalition government had been captured by the fossil-fuel industry is the sad fate of Malcolm Turnbull. In August 2015, to the great relief of most of the country, Turnbull successfully challenged Abbott for the party leadership and became our fifth prime minister since 2007, sixth if we count Rudd twice. Abbott had become a joke, eating raw onions and knighting Prince Philip. Turnbull was a good communicator and promised leadership that respected the intelligence of the Australian people. "We need advocacy, not slogans," he said, when he announced his challenge. He also said that he would retain the Coalition's policy on climate change and its commitment to a plebiscite on same-sex marriage rather than a parliamentary vote. Turnbull believed in neither of these things. He was able to steer same-sex marriage to a satisfactory conclusion. Shifting the Coalition on climate change defeated him entirely. As well as trying to appease the climate deniers and sceptics inside his own party, Turnbull's hands were tied by his agreement with the Nationals. After a leadership change in one of their parties, the Liberals and Nationals renegotiated their Coalition agreement. Although this has never been made public, it is widely believed that then Nationals leader Barnaby Joyce included a commitment to retain the Coalition's climate policy.

Turnbull made two attempts to legislate a framework for the energy market which would encourage new investment and enable Australia to meet its Paris target of a 26 per cent cut in carbon emissions from 2005 levels. The first attempt was the Clean Energy Target, which was one of the recommendations of a review by Chief Scientist Alan Finkel. This looked much too much like the renewable energy target for Tony Abbott and his anti-climateers in the Coalition. It was, said Abbott, "a tax on coal."

So Turnbull dropped it and he and Energy Minister Josh Frydenberg came up with the National Energy Guarantee (NEG). This would put a premium on affordability and reliability, but also included obligations to reduce emissions and legislate the Paris target. The NEG passed the Liberal party room, though not unanimously, and opponents threatened to cross the floor. At the start of the second-last week of August 2018, Turnbull took out the emissions reduction target, but it was too late, and by the end of the week he was gone. Turnbull knew the terrible risk the world was running in not reducing emissions fast; he knew that the smart money was moving away from coal; he knew opportunities for innovation and investment in renewable energy were being missed. But as prime minister of Australia, he was unable to act on this knowledge. Nothing would satisfy the anti-climateers short of a wholehearted commitment to the future of coal.

COAL COUNTRY

At the gala dinner in March this year to celebrate the centenary of the Nationals, federal president Larry Anthony boasted that the party played a key role in twice removing Malcolm Turnbull because of his climate change policy. The Coalition had won the 2019 election against the odds, but not the seat of Richmond on the north coast of New South Wales, which had voted three generations of the Anthony family into parliament, including Larry. The demography of this once predominantly agricultural area has shifted, with sea-changers and alternatives moving into the coastal towns, and the seat has been held by Labor since 2004 with substantial support from the Greens. To survive, the Nationals needed new supporters and they were finding them in the coalminers of central Queensland. Whatever the contribution Bill Shorten's unpopularity, franking credits or negative gearing may have made to the Coalition winning in 2019, the brutal truth is that Labor lost the election in Queensland and it lost it in large part because of the Queensland Liberal National Party's successful weaponising of coal.

When he was forced to stand aside in mid-2017 because of doubts about his mother's citizenship, Queensland Nationals senator Matt Canavan posted an extraordinary statement on Facebook: "It has been such an honour to represent the Australian mining sector over the past year. It is an industry full of fine, hard-working and innovative people. Mining and resources are a uniquely Australian success story. From the small, gambling explorers and prospectors to the large, world-beating multi-nationals, the industry provides rich and diverse experiences that can take you to the smallest towns of outback Australia to the biggest cities in the world." Nowhere did he mention the farmers his party was formed to serve, nor that many farmers are challenging mining's social licence, fighting tooth and nail to protect their agricultural land from mining.

The National Party's leadership has close links to the resources industry. Past leaders Mark Vaile and John Anderson made fortunes out of resources after leaving politics; Matt Canavan's brother John is an enthusiastic investor in Queensland coal assets; Larry Anthony has lobbied for the Chinese mining giant Shenhua's Watermark coalmine on the edge of the Liverpool Plains in New South Wales, which is opposed by the local farming communities. In March 2019, on Network 10's *The Project*, Waleed Aly asked Nationals leader Michael McCormack, "Could you name a single, big policy area where the Nats have sided with the interests of farmers over the interests of miners when they come into conflict?" Off the top of his head, McCormack could not name one.

The National Party has become the party of coal. Malcolm Turnbull tells in *A Bigger Picture* of a meeting that included Nationals George Christensen, Keith Pitt, Barnaby Joyce and Andrew Gee, who were arguing that a new coal-fired power station would deliver cheaper power. "Okay, I asked, what coal price are you assuming? They didn't know. How much coal will the new coal plant use for each megawatt hour? Again they didn't know. How much do you think the new plant will cost? No idea. I was patient and polite as I explained the economics of a new coal-fired power station and how it was no longer competitive with renewables plus storage to deliver dispatchable power. They weren't convinced." No doubt they were infuriated by Turnbull's somewhat condescending interrogation, but, as Bridget McKenzie told him on the way out, "You can't reason with them, PM. It's religion. They don't care about the numbers." But they do care about electoral numbers.

The National Party's political power depends on the geographical concentration of its vote. At the 2019 election, it won a little less than 7 per cent of first preference votes, if we attribute to it a quarter of the vote of the Queensland Liberal National Party (LNP), which was formed in 2008 from a merger of the Queensland branches of the two parties. With this vote, the Nationals won fifteen seats. By contrast, the Greens' national first preference vote of more than 10 per cent is diffused across electorates, and they have only one lonely representative in the House of Representatives. As another geographically concentrated activity, mining offers the

Nationals a tantalising way to supplement their declining agricultural electoral base.

In the weeks before the 2019 election, Bob Brown led a convoy to #StopAdani through central Queensland that was met with jeering hostility, enabling the LNP to mobilise regional loyalties. Shorten equivocated on whether or not Labor would review the mine's environmental approval if it won government, sowing distrust among both supporters and opponents of the mine. Making Adani a key electoral issue was the last thing Labor needed as it tried to reconcile environmentally concerned city voters with regional voters who believed their economic futures depended on coalmining. It couldn't be done, so the best thing for Labor was to keep voters' minds focused on issues like health and education. Instead, Shorten kept being asked where he stood on Adani and was never able to give a clear answer. Clive Palmer, who has substantial coal interests in the Galilee Basin, spent $60 million on advertising his United Australia Party. Although the party won no seats, Palmer was well satisfied with the result. His Shifty Shorten ads, he said, had succeeded in preventing a Labor victory.

In all states and territories except for Queensland and Western Australia, Labor plus left independents won the majority of seats. In Western Australia, it won only five to the Coalition's eleven, the same as in 2016, but in Queensland it lost two seats, leaving it with only six of the state's thirty seats. As well, sitting LNP members enjoyed massive swings. "I never expected numbers like these," Michelle Landry told the ABC on election night. "Thank you, Bob Brown, is all I can say. He came up here trying to tell Queenslanders what we should and shouldn't be doing, and it actually drew together the agricultural and mining sectors."

Landry is the member for Capricornia, which stretches along the coast from Rockhampton in the south to the southern suburbs of Mackay. In the north and west it includes major mining centres such as the coalmining town of Collinsville, where the LNP wants a new coal-fired power station built. For most of its history, Capricornia has been Labor. Landry won the seat in 2016 with a margin of just 0.6 per cent. In 2019, the margin was

12.4 per cent. The miners had deserted Labor, and not just in Queensland, but also in the NSW coalmining electorate of Hunter, where the primary vote of the sitting Labor member, Joel Fitzgibbon, dropped by almost 15 per cent.

In Queensland, said Canavan, there had been "a hi-vis workers' revolution," with the extreme demands of climate change activists "pushing what have otherwise been strong Labor-voting areas towards the conservative side of politics."

When the Country Party was established to represent farmers and people living in country towns, it was informed by what the political scientist Don Aitkin called "country-mindedness," the belief that country folk were more independent, hard-working and morally authentic than people living easy, pleasure-seeking lives in the cities. The self-indulgent Greens-voting inner city versus the hard-working regions is the most recent iteration of the opposition between city and country that has shaped Australian politics for at least 100 years. Here is Canavan in February this year, a few days after he resigned from cabinet to support Joyce's leadership challenge to McCormack:

> Our wealth producing industries, like farming, mining and manufacturing, have never been under greater attack. Farmers have had their land rights stripped off them, dams are stopped because of some snail or frog and mines get sabotaged by rich, city-based whingers who threaten and bully law-abiding businesses.

Get it? Australia's wealth is produced outside the cities and the cities are full of whingeing green bullies. This rhetoric is designed to pull regional voters back to the Nationals.

Canavan is fairly restrained. Fellow Queensland National George Christensen is the party specialist in anti-green invective. In 2014, he described environmentalists opposed to the expansion of Adani's port at Abbot Point as "gutless green grubs"; in 2018, he posted a photo on Facebook of himself aiming a handgun with the caption, "You gotta ask yourself, do you feel lucky greenie punks." Christensen draws on the anti-green invective in circulation since the battles in Tasmania over the forests.

As well as maintaining their political relevance, the Nationals' specialisation in coal advocacy helps the Liberals, who can't afford to be as openly hostile to environmentally concerned voters as the Nationals are. Like Labor, they are threatened by Greens and independents in city electorates. Independent Zali Steggall stood against Tony Abbott in Warringah on a platform of climate action and won.

The Queensland Nationals successfully weaponised coal in the 2019 election. Even though this was as much a strategy for the party's political survival as it was a matter of conviction, it is further evidence of the fossil-fuel lobby's success. Without Abbott, the Liberal Party could not be relied on, but with the junior partner turning itself into the party of coal, fossil fuels could be sure of a seat at the cabinet table of a Coalition government.

SUPERPOWER OR PARIAH?

I began this essay with the bushfires, and the question of why so many of Australia's politicians are still denying the dangers of a heating planet and resisting what we must do to protect the futures of our children and grandchildren. The answer I have explored is the continuing dependence of Australia on the farm and the quarry for export income, and the successful capture of so many of our politicians by the fossil-fuel lobby – mostly on the Coalition side of politics, but Labor has not been immune.

I showed the way Australia's success in exporting first wool and then minerals created an economy with a dual economic structure, in which the industries earning our export income produced far fewer jobs than the sectors producing goods and services for domestic consumption. For most of the twentieth century, protected manufacturing for the home market was a big employer, but it was inefficient and uncompetitive by world standards. When it did start to compete, it was too late and is now in poor shape. The big employers are health care and social assistance, retail, accommodation, hospitality and education. Tourism and international students gave an export focus to the service sector.

The mining industry cannot be blamed directly for the weakness of Australian manufacturing, even though its success drove the dollar higher and undermined manufacturing's competitiveness. The blame lies mainly with political elites of both sides of politics, who waited too long to dismantle Australia's protective tariffs. Once the most recent resources boom roared into life, most of our leaders gave manufacturing little thought.

It is climate change that has turned the dependence of Australia's export income on minerals into a curse, and not all minerals. As renewable energy sources are developed, we can continue to export iron ore, bauxite, gold and other non-fossil-fuel minerals without contributing to the rise in global temperatures. It is only coal and gas we will have to give up and it is the fossil-fuel lobby that has turned our dependence on minerals into a political curse.

The fossil-fuel lobby has benefited greatly from the polarised politics of the last three decades. It is a moot point when this polarisation started. Some put it in 1975, with the ill will flowing from the Dismissal, but I think the current period of discord began when Keating was prime minister. Brilliant at invective, he sharpened up lines of division around race and Indigenous politics and Howard transformed these into the culture wars.

When serious pressure began at the turn of the century for governments to reduce carbon emissions, many cultural warriors transformed smoothly into climate warriors. Although the issues were very different, the enemies were mostly the same, which for many politicians is what counts. The fossil-fuel lobby deliberately stoked the polarisation, fostered climate change denialism among Australia's conservative political elites, and rewarded its political advocates with jobs. But it could not have created the climate wars so easily without the preceding culture wars.

The culture wars were less destructive of our national politics than the climate wars have been because they had little to do with economics. Howard could introduce an economic reform like the GST, and try to reform industrial relations, even as he denounced black armband history. The climate wars are different because they are about what we export and how we produce the energy that drives our economy and they have made it impossible for successive Coalition governments to sustain a coherent economic narrative to support reform. The past fifteen years of climate wars have, in the words of Alan Kohler, "ruined Australia's ability to conduct any kind of sensible discussion about economic policy and to achieve consensus on anything."

The climate warriors' support for coal and gas depends on a cascading series of arguments. The first is that the planet is not heating so there is no need to cut fossil-fuel emissions; second, even if it is, it is not caused by humans; third, even if it is, Australia's emissions from both what we burn and what we export are so small that stopping them won't make any difference; fourth, the drug dealer's defence: if we don't sell the coal and gas, someone else will; fifth, the predicted damage will not be that bad and doesn't warrant the economic costs. The commentator Greg Sheridan even argued that if "these crook environmental outcomes are going to come about anyway, would you rather confront them as rich people or as poor people?" The first two and fifth are refuted by science, the rest by both ethics and by political realism. We cannot expect other countries to allow us to escape contributing to the global effort to reduce emissions without some sort of payback.

Australia's fossil-fuel curse operates through the nexus of economic and political power and both aspects are now under pressure. The price of renewable energy has fallen faster than expected, and storage technology developed more quickly. Renewable energy is now a market disrupter with a logic of its own, as the new technologies of solar, wind, electric vehicles and lithium-ion batteries disrupt global energy and transport markets. This, says Tim Buckley from the Institute for Energy Economics and Financial Analysis, is "why we've seen ten coal plant closures in the last ten years in Australia. New coal plant builds are not economically viable nor bankable." Since the pandemic, thermal coal prices have fallen by around 30 per cent. At this price, many existing and planned mines are unprofitable, including Adani. Gas, too, is under threat. Building the expensive infrastructure needed to extract gas is a long-term investment and future returns are looking uncertain.

Capital is deserting fossil fuels, in part because renewables and falling prices are threatening future returns, but also because of shareholder and customer campaigns for banks and superannuation funds to divest from fossil fuels. There are countless examples. Adani has so far been unable to find a single bank willing to fund its Carmichael mine in Queensland's Galilee Basin, and three of Australia's big four banks have pledged to stop lending to thermal coal projects.

Earlier this year, BlackRock, the world's largest fund manager, announced that it was putting climate change at the centre of its investment strategy and off-loading its thermal coal shares. Whether or not it was doing this for environmental reasons or just for risk management, the effect is the same. Economist John Quiggin describes it as "the canary in the coal-mine," with big implications for the Australian government. Once bond investors follow BlackRock's lead, divestment of Australian government bonds will follow, he predicts. Sweden has already decided to sell its Australian government bonds. At Woodside's 2020 AGM in April, more than half of the shareholders backed motions to commit to hard targets to reduce direct and indirect emissions. The motions, framed by ethical investment group the Australasian Centre for Corporate Responsibility, were not supported by Woodside's Board, but they succeeded nevertheless.

The pandemic seems to have intensified capital's flight, perhaps because of the slump in coal prices as the global economy shrinks. Perhaps also because powerful people now realise that some long-predicted disasters do in fact happen. In April, Japan's three largest institutional banks announced they would no longer finance new coal-fired power. One, Mizuho, had been the world's largest private financier of coal. Allianz, one of the world's largest insurers, said it would no longer invest in coal or insure it. Tim Buckley reports that 133 large financial institutions announced their exit from coal in the last two weeks of April.

A further political risk is from government action against carbon-intensive economies. Robert Gottliebsen, who writes a business column in *The Australian* and is by no means a green leftie, warns that, in his judgment, carbon-based tariffs are ahead: "Business models in most industries are set to change, driven by three forces: government regulation, community demand and, perhaps most important of all, the allocation of capital away from carbon-based companies." Even Australia's very own Vicar of Bray, journalist Paul Kelly, who is never far from the orthodoxies of the powerful, has written that the Morrison government's problem with climate change is the risk of being boycotted by global capital and marginalised. Kelly was predicting more decisive global action after the now-postponed conference in Glasgow in November, where British prime minister Boris Johnson was foreshadowing requiring every country to outline how it will reach net zero emissions by 2050.

In Australia, the nexus is also under pressure from community activism. Since 2010, an alliance of local environmental, community and farming groups calling itself "Lock the Gate" has been opposing coal and coal seam gas developments, mainly in New South Wales and Queensland, but also in the other states and the Northern Territory. Its mission is "to protect Australia's natural, cultural and agricultural resources from inappropriate mining and to educate and empower all Australians to demand sustainable solutions to food and energy production." It calls on landowners to "lock the gate" to prevent access to their land by gas companies and to refuse to negotiate the sale of their properties to coal companies.

"Lock the Gate" is a challenge to fossil-fuel companies' social licence from the heart of Australia's farming country: Queensland's Darling Downs, New South Wales' Liverpool Plains, Victoria's Gippsland. These are David and Goliath contests, with small producers tackling the corporate giants, but as a new political formation the coalition of farmers and environmentalists has been remarkably successful. Community protests have succeeded in having licences withdrawn or abandoned, and in forcing more stringent reviews. Except for Queensland, the other states and territories have imposed restrictions on coal seam gas exploration and development – although some, like the Northern Territory's moratorium on fracking, have proved to be temporary.

Also driving capital's desertion of fossil fuels is the attractiveness of renewables as an investment. At present in Australia, this is being stalled by uncertainty over the Coalition's energy policy, but the potential is starting to be recognised more generally. In 2019, Ross Garnaut published *Superpower: Australia's low-carbon opportunity*. In it, he argues that Australia can become a renewable energy superpower. Our climate gives us a natural advantage in the production of renewable energy. With the cheapest energy in the world, minerals and food can be processed here rather than shipped off raw and then reimported. Australia could expand its production of steel (using renewable energy to make hydrogen), aluminium, silicon and ammonia. These would be located close to the sources of the minerals in regional Australia and could easily replace the relatively few jobs lost in mining fossil fuels, which should allay the Nationals' concerns about regional employment. It would also reduce transport costs. Australia would have both reinvigorated, employment-rich manufacturing and new export industries.

It's a brilliant strategy, giving Australia a new source of export income to replace that lost from fossil fuels, re-starting manufacturing and providing jobs in the regions. What Garnaut shows is that action on climate change can create enormous economic opportunities. The competing goods of the economy and environment – a mainstay of arguments against environmental protection – need compete no longer.

As strong as the forces working against Australia's fossil-fuel producers are, the carbon lobby still has considerable power over state and federal governments, though the emphasis has shifted from coal to gas. Addressing the National Press Club in January this year, Prime Minister Morrison said, "We need to get the gas from under our feet. There is no credible energy transition plan, for an economy like Australia, in particular, that does not involve the greater use of gas as an important transition fuel." Just days later, he announced an agreement with the NSW state government to invest $1 billion in emissions-reduction initiatives, in return for matching funding from the state and the removal of barriers to expanding gas supply. In his sights was Santos's gas project at Narrabri in north-west New South Wales, where Santos wants to drill 850 natural gas wells on around 425 sites, mainly in the Pilliga state forest, but also on some private agricultural land.

Promoting gas as a transitional fuel between coal and renewables at least admits the need for a transition, and a decade or so ago, when renewables were more expensive, gas was widely seen as a plausible way to reduce emissions. But renewables are now much cheaper and although gas emits 50 per cent less carbon dioxide than coal, its extraction releases methane, which makes a greater contribution to heating the planet than carbon dioxide. Then there are the political costs of pushing gas extraction into settled regional communities and destroying good agricultural land.

While everyone is focused on the pandemic and parliaments are suspended, government decisions to expand coalmining and gas extraction have been slipped through. The NSW government has approved the extension of coalmining operations under the Woronora reservoir, which supplies some of Sydney's drinking water. The Victorian government has lifted its moratorium on conventional gas mining, though kept it on fracking. In Queensland, Premier Annastacia Palaszczuk welcomed Arrow Energy's decision to press ahead with its Surat gas project as "fantastic news" and promised an "accelerated works program" for when we come out of this crisis. The project is only promising 200 jobs after construction, which need to be set against jobs risked in other sectors, especially in farming on the fertile floodplains above the gas. Nor did she mention that the local community has been fighting this project since 2014, because "this temporary and destructive project poses significant risk to the long-term food security of Queensland."

With the pandemic having paused so much of the world's economy, it feels as though Australia is at a crossroads. We have the chance to shake off the curse of fossil fuels, but equally probable is that our leaders will stick with what they know and eschew innovation, like the men of the early 1960s, when Donald Horne complained that decades of tariff protection had produced a "look-no-brains attitude." The signs are it will be more business as usual than embrace of the new.

Morrison appointed a National COVID-19 Coordination Commission to advise on how to mitigate the economic and social effects of the pandemic, but the commission's lack of transparency and accountability is concerning. There is no enabling legislation, nor any public information on how members were appointed, how it will operate, to whom it will report and when, and whether its recommendations will be made public. The opacity surrounding the commission is evidence of Morrison's authoritarian tendencies. These served him well during the early days of the crisis, when swift decisions were needed, but are much less well suited to managing complex conflicts of interest and ideas about how to rebuild our economy.

Even more concerning for the subject of this essay is that the handpicked membership is skewed towards people with links to fossil fuels. There is no one from the employment-rich sectors of tourism, hospitality, education, arts and entertainment, nor from the burgeoning renewable energy sector. The chairman, Nev Power, is a former managing director and CEO of Fortescue Metals and was a director and major shareholder of the oil and gas company Strike Energy at the time of his appointment. After criticism of an apparent conflict of interest, he has since stepped back from an active role with the company, but this has not quieted concerns. After all, he will still have the same mindset. Another member of the small committee, Catherine Tanna, also has a background in fossil fuels, as does the co-opted special adviser on manufacturing, Andrew Liveris, whose draft report advocates government support for the development of gas to provide cheap energy to manufacturing. The report gave no consideration to renewables as alternative sources of energy, nor did it mention climate change or the financial risks of renewables disrupting the energy market. Were its recommendations to be acted on, this would be evidence that the federal Coalition government is still as captive to the fossil-fuel industry as it was in Howard's day, but this is to get ahead of ourselves. Public concern about climate change is as strong as when Howard was in government, the financial calculations are much more favourable to renewables, and business leaders are more aware of the risks of a heating planet.

In a speech to a Clean Energy Council forum in May, Innes Willox, the chief executive of the Australian Industry Group, linked restoring growth after the pandemic to making a successful transition to net zero emissions by 2050. "Our national interest lies in global action to avoid as much climate change as possible." A bipartisan climate policy can help the economy recover by supporting investment to build a zero-emissions economy. There is much more agreement over climate change than we think, he said: it is the politics that have been the problem.

Faced with the crisis of a global pandemic, for the first time in more than a decade Australia has had evidence-based, bipartisan policy-making. Politicians have listened to the scientists and not hesitated to inflict economic pain on their advice. A Liberal prime minister has worked effectively with both Labor and Liberal premiers and together they have achieved remarkable results, protecting us from the trauma COVID-19 has brought to other countries. To do this, they put ideology and the protection of vested interests aside and behaved like adults. Can they do the same to commit to fast and effective action to try to save our children's and grandchildren's future, to prevent the catastrophic fires and heatwaves the scientists predict, the species extinction and the famines? After all, governments are our risk managers of last resort.

SOURCES

1 "Our emissions reduction policies": Scott Morrison, press conference, 2 January 2020.

3 "We weren't listened to": *On Breakfast with Wendy Harmer and Robbie Buck*, ABC Radio Sydney, 3 January 2020.

5 "should be proud": Angus Taylor, "We should be proud of our climate change efforts", *The Australian*, 1 January 2020.

6 "The international community": "COP25: UN chief laments lost opportunity as climate talks end", SBS News (online), 16 December 2019.

6 "caught in a climate spiral": Robinson Meyer, "Australia will lose to Climate Change", *The Atlantic*, 4 January 2020.

9 "vying with iron ore": Statistics Section, Office of Economic Analysis, Investment & Economic Division, *Australia's Trade Since Federation*, Department of Foreign Affairs and Trade, Canberra, Chart 7.

9 "these three earned": Statistics Section, Trade and Investment Economics Branch, Office of the Chief Economist, *Australia's Top 25 Exports, Goods and Services, (a), (A$ Million)*, Department of Foreign Affairs and Trade, 19 December 2019.

9 "world's third-largest exporter": International Energy Agency figures reported in Nick Kilvert, "Australia is the world's third-largest exporter of CO2 in fossil fuels, report finds", ABC Science (online), 19 August 2019.

12 "Australia is rich, dumb": Aaron Patrick, "Australia is rich, dumb and getting dumber", *Australian Financial Review*, 8 October 2019.

12 "Just over 7 per cent" and other employment figures throughout the essay: "Australia: Industry sector of employment", Labor Market Information Portal, last quarter 2019; .id website, accessed 13 May 2020 at https://profile.id.com.au/australia/industries.

13 "For mining companies": Nick Toscano, "Rise of the machines", *The Age*, 30 November 2019.

13 "It's not many jobs": Rod Campbell, "Fact check: Will Adani's coal mine really boost employment by 10,000 jobs?", *Business Spectator*, *The Australian*, 31 August 2015.

13 "not many jobs in coalmining": RMIT ABC Fact Check, "Are there really 54,000 people employed in thermal coal mining?", ABC News (online), 11 July 2019, updated 27 September 2019.

13 "about 44,000 people": Productivity Commission, *Australia's Automotive Manufacturing Industry*, Productivity Commission Inquiry Report, No. 70, 31 March 2014, p. 6.

15 "In 1950": Australian Bureau of Statistics, "The wool industry – looking back and forward", 1301.0 *Year Book Australia* – 2003, Canberra, ABS, 24 January 2003.

16 "less than 1 per cent": "Australia's top 25 exports, goods and services", Canberra, DFAT, 2019.

17 "In 1963–64": Department of Foreign Affairs and Trade, *Fifty Years of Australia's Trade*, DFAT, Canberra, accessed 14 May 2020 at www.dfat.gov.au/sites/default/files/fifty-years-of-Australias-trade.pdf, p. 3.

17 "In 2003": Index Mundi, "Coal, Australian thermal coal, monthly price – US dollars per metric ton", Index Mundi website, accessed 13 May 2020, www.indexmundi.com/commodities/?commodity=coal-australian&months=300.

18 "a little more than 9 per cent": Geoscience Australian, "Black Coal", *Australian Atlas of Minerals Resources, Mines & Processing Centres*, accessed 13 May 2020 at www.australianminesatlas.gov.au/aimr/commodity/black_coal.html#world_ranking.

18 "This rose": CEIC, "Australia Coal Production", accessed 13 May 2020 at www.ceicdata.com/en/indicator/australia/coal-production.

19 "By 2012": Woodside Energy, "The North West Shelf Project – Twenty-five years of LNG export", video posted to YouTube, 10 November 2014, accessed 13 May 2020 at www.youtube.com/watch?v=1UnP11W1Kog&list=PLPBvAvlDsL4jaaOrXz_xJf5copPY_p9vj+.

19 "the largest concentration": Bechtel, "Curtis Island LNG, Queensland, Australia", Bechtel website, accessed 13 May 2020 at www.bechtel.com/projects/curtis-island-lng/.

24 "By 1940–41": Australian Bureau of Statistics, "Development of manufacturing industries in Australia", 1301.0 – *Year Book Australia*, 1988, ABS, Canberra, 1 January 1988.

24 "Boris Schedvin": "The Australian economy on the hinge of history", *The Australian Economic Review*, March 1987, p. 22.

25 "it peaked": Australian Bureau of Statistics, "Industry Structure and Performance", 1301.0 *Year Book of Australia*, 2012, ABS, Canberra.

25 "only around 6 per cent": Reserve Bank of Australia, "Composition of the Australian economy snapshot", RBA, 11 May 2020.

26 "77 per cent": Government Offices of Sweden, *Smart Industry: A strategy for new industrialisation for Sweden*, Ministry of Enterprise and Innovation, p. 6.

27 "a look-no-brains attitude", "The processes of invention": Donald Horne, *The Lucky Country: Australia in the sixties*, Angus & Robertson Classics edition, 1978, p. 119.

27 "a stupid society": Horne, *The Lucky Country*, p. 128.

27 "How often have we": Quoted in J.R. Nethercote, "The Vernon report: Hits, misses and Menzies' reaction", *The Sydney Morning Herald*, 5 October 2015.

28 "tariffs averaged": Michael Emmery, *Australian Manufacturing: A brief history of industry policy and trade liberalisation*, Research Paper 7, 1999–2000, Australian Parliamentary Library, 19 October 1999, p. 6.

28 "tariff of 57.5 per cent": David Richardson, *Protection in the Motor Vehicle Industry*, Current Issues Brief 22, 1996–97, Australian Parliamentary Library.

30 "We took the view": *Australian Financial Review*, 15 May 1986, pp. 8–9, reproduced in Richard H. Snape, Lisa Gropp & Tas Luttrell (eds), *Australian Trade Policy 1965–1997: A documentary history*, St Leonards, NSW, Allen & Unwin, 1998, pp. 48–9.

30 "In 1987": Ross Garnaut, *Australia and the Northeast Asian Ascendancy: Report to the prime minister and the minister of foreign affairs and trade*, Canberra, AGPS, p. 54.

31 "was sceptical": John Button, *As It Happened*, Melbourne, Text Publishing, 1999, p. 324

31 "This is a young": Quoted in Button, pp. 341–2.

32 "top ten export": Steve Bracks, *Review of Australia's Automotive Industry*, Department of Innovation, Industry, Science and Research, July 2008, p. 9.

32 "By 1992": Treasury submission to House of Representatives Economics, Finance and Public Administration Committee public inquiry, August 1996.

32 "For the last two decades": House of Representatives Standing Committee on Economics, Finance and Public Administration, *Australian Manufacturing Today and Tomorrow: Inquiring into the state of Australia's manufactured export and import competing base now and beyond the resources boom*, Commonwealth of Australia, Canberra, July 2007, p. xxi.

33 "Just under 12 per cent": Malcolm Edey, *The Australian Economy in 2007*, address to the Australian Industry Group, Economy 2007, Sydney, 7 March 2007, graph 10, accessed 13 May 2020 at www.rba.gov.au/speeches/2007/sp-ag-070307.html.

33 "In 2018": Department of Industry, Science, Energy and Resources, *The Australian economy in 2017*, Industry Insights No. 1, June 2018, Table 2.1.

35 "I never want": Kevin Rudd, speech reproduced in *The Sydney Morning Herald*, 27 June 2013.

37 "having difficulty": Ben Peckham, "French tell subs firms to shape up", *The Australian*, 13 February 2020.

37 "the highly advanced": Karen Andrews, "Industry consortium to manufacture 2000 ventilators", media release, 9 April 2020.

38 "domestic economic sovereignty", "an open trading nation": Scott Morrison, press conference, 7 April 2020.

41 "so that school children": G.K. Ken; "Outline of Public Relations Programme for the Australian Mining Industry Council, International Public Relations", unpublished paper, 16 May 1972, cited in Kosmas Tsokhas, "The Australian Mining Industry Council 1967–75", *Business History*, 40/3, July 1998, p. 123.

41 "Politicians can only accept": Cited in Dominic Kelly, *Political Troglodytes and Economic Lunatics: The Hard Right in Australia*, Black Inc., Carlton, 2019, p. 43.

48 "We all write the same way": Quoted in Guy Pearse, *High and Dry: John Howard, climate change and the selling of Australia's future*, Penguin, Richmond, 2007, p. 347, note 645.

49 "were deeply concerned", Lavoisier, "About the Lavoisier Group", Lavoisier website, August 2008, accessed 16 March 2020 at www.lavoisier.com.au/lavoisier-about.php.

49–50 "The Environmentalists": *Quadrant*, July 1989, p. 18, cited in Kelly, *Political Troglodytes*, p. 165.

50 "about five minutes", etc.: Quoted in Kelly, *Political Troglodytes*, p. 166.

50 "to appease": *Confessions of a Failed Finance Minister*, p. 208, cited in Kelly, *Political Troglodytes*, p. 169.

51 "a comical degree of self-confidence": Robert Manne, *Bad News: Murdoch's Australian and the Shaping of the Nation*, Quarterly Essay 43, September 2011, pp. 51–2.

52 "there was an understanding": Guy Pearse, *Quarry Vision: Coal, climate change and the end of the resource boom*, Quarterly Essay 33, March 2009, p. 44.

53 "it was not the environment": Martin Gelin, "The Misogyny of Climate Deniers", *New Republic*, 29 August 2019; Jonas Anshelm and Martine Hultman, "A Green Fatwa? Climate change as a threat to the masculinity of industrial modernity", *International Journal of Masculinity Studies*, Vol. 9, No. 2, 2014, pp. 84–96.

53 "There is no room for bipartisanship": *AFR* Energy Summit, 10 October 2018.

54 "You should keep": *Q&A*, ABC (TV), 3 February 2020.

55 "Lowy Institute opinion poll": Allan Gyngell, *Australia and the World: Public opinion and foreign policy*, The Lowy Institute Poll 2007, Sydney, Lowy Institute, 2007.

55 "Howard admitted": "perfect storm" in 2013 lecture to the Global Warming Policy Foundation http://www.thegwpf.org/content/uploads/2013/12/Howard-2013-Annual-GWPF-Lecture.pdf

57 "whether you're": Paul Cleary, *Too Much Luck: The Mining Boom and Australia's Future*, Black Inc., Melbourne, 2011, p. 78.

58 "According to Ross Garnaut": Ross Garnaut, *Superpower: Australia's low-carbon opportunity*, Black Inc., Carlton, 2019, p. 32.

57–8 "This episode highlights" and "as long as there is breath": Cleary, *Too Much Luck*, p. 82.

58 "Along comes a carbon tax.": Credlin, *Sunday Agenda*, Sky News, 12 February 2020.

59 "After meeting with Gore": Garnaut, *Superpower*, p. 33.

59 "declined by around 14 per cent": Tim Dodd, "R&D spending drops below OECD average", *The Australian*, 25 September 2019.

60 "a tax on coal": Katharine Murphy and Gareth Hutchens, "Tony Abbott fears Finkel's clean energy target could be a 'magic pudding'", *The Guardian*, 12 June 2017.

62 "It has been such an honour": Matt Canavan, Facebook, 27 July 2017.

63 "Okay, I asked", "You can't reason with them": Malcolm Turnbull, *A Bigger Picture*, Hardie Grant, Sydney, 2020, pp. 608–9.

63 "At the 2019 election": Outside Queensland the Nationals vote was 4.51 per cent. The LNP vote was 8.67 and delivered 22 seats, of which 5 can be ascribed to the Nationals on the basis of members sitting in the Nationals' party room.

64 "succeeded in preventing": "Election 2019: Clive Palmer says Scott Morrison can thank UAP's anti-Labor ads for result", ABC News (online), 19 May 2019.

64 "I never expected": Allyson Horn, "Election results: Why Queensland turned its back on Labor and helped Scott Morrison to victory", ABC News (online), 19 May 2019.

65 "a hi-vis workers' revolution": David Wroe, "Matt Canvan hails 'workers' revolution' as Queensland savages Labor", *The Sydney Morning Herald*, 19 May 2019.

65 "Our wealth producing": Matt Canavan, Facebook, 7 February 2020.

68 "ruined Australia's ability": Alan Kohler, "Reform agenda amid the coronavirus pandemic? Give us a break", *The Australian*, 27 April 2020.

69 "these crook environmental outcomes": *The Australian*, 20 June 2014.

69 "why we've seen": Tim Buckley, "IEEFA Update: Renewable energy could leave USD20 trillion of fossil fuel assets stranded within 30 years", Institute for Energy Economics and Financial Analysis, IEEFA website, 5 March 2020.

70 "the canary in the coalmine": John Quiggin, "BlackRock is the canary in the coalmine", *The Conversation*, 16 January 2020.

70 "not supported": Nick Toscano, "Breakthrough Moment", *The Age*, 30 April 2020.

70 "133 large financial institutions": Bob Carr, "Coal exodus continues unablated", *The Age*, 15 May 2020, p. 23.

70 "Kelly was predicting": *The Australian*, 19 February 2020.

71 "to protect": Lock the Gate, "About us", Lock the Gate website, accessed 13 May 2020.

72 "We need to get the gas": Scott Morrison, Address to the National Press Club, Canberra, 28 January 2020.

73 "fantastic news": "Arrow Energy announces $10bn Surat Gas project in Queensland", Sky News Australia, 17 April 2020.

73 "this temporary and destructive project": Lock the Gate, "Palaszczuk government's Arrow Energy admiration misses the mark, condemns farmers", Lock the Gate website, 17 April 2020.

73 "draft report": Adam Morton, "Leaked Covid-19 commission report calls for Australian taxpayers to underwrite gas industry expansion", *The Guardian*, 21 May 2020.

74 "Our national interest lies": Innes Willox, Speech to the Stimulus Summit: A Renewables-Led Economic Recovery, online event, 6 May 2020.

CRY ME A RIVER

Correspondence

Maryanne Slattery

Margaret Simons' essay is an evocative account of a moment. From the title it is clear that she did not find, and does not foresee, a happy ending. The Basin Plan has been around in some form since 2007. Many players have been telling a version of the same narrative for longer. Participants jostle for position and power to control, or at least influence, the future. But it is apparent from the essay that the imagined future is a version of the past. By chance the essay is a record of the last days before the COVID-19 pandemic. Now, in the words of Paul Valéry, "the future is not what it used to be." What stands out from Simons' essay is that so few of the people with a claim to managing the Basin gave any hint of what they might do if the future threw up something unexpected, such as a pandemic. Climate change will be a greater challenge still.

Simons' view is personal, compassionate, unsentimental and moving. It is clear-eyed and tough – she sees the spin and self-interest, the obsession with process that serves only to delay. And it is harsh where harshness is the only proper response. She has a gift of giving enough of the politics to make it clear and interesting and keeping it relevant to where we are now. She says one of her aims in the essay is "to rescue the Basin's narratives from the abstract." She has achieved this. Her essay is the opposite of the desiccated language of the water managers.

From among the competing narratives she paints a bigger story of the Basin. She gets quickly and clearly to the interlocking influences that contribute to "the wonder and the awfulness of our attempts to manage it." Phillip Glyde's analogy is that the Plan is like upgrading an inefficient petrol combustion engine. He seems to argue that perfect shouldn't be the enemy of good and we should instead strive for continual improvement. It's a misleading analogy that suggests the many reviews identified by Simons are proactive and planned. She correctly observes that they rarely question the fundamentals, because they are mostly undertaken in response to external pressure and are intended to defend. For example, the review of water markets by the Australian Competition and Consumer Commission (ACCC) is unlikely to question their underlying premise, as the ACCC was instrumental in their design. Mick Keelty published a report to "bring better governance and transparency" in his capacity as Interim Inspector-General of the Murray–Darling Basin, in which he didn't mention unmanaged floodplain harvesting or the much-criticised water efficiency program. To return to Glyde's engine analogy, that is like overlooking the fact that your engine has no fuel tank. Too often, the Murray–Darling Basin Authority chooses and pays the reviewer, designs the terms of reference and edits the final report. Co-operative "independent reviewers" become the go-to experts for future reviews. It's a lucrative business.

Criticism is denied, discredited or ignored. For example, the South Australian royal commission, which the Commonwealth refused to participate in, was wrong according to the Authority and politically motivated according to Minister David Littleproud.

Public commentary is classified as "pro–Basin Plan" or "anti–Basin Plan." In this binary discussion, challenges to the status quo are unwelcome. Pointing out that hundreds of millions of dollars have been spent on non-existent water, or that the government withholds key documents, is interpreted as meaning one wants to rip up the Plan. Reporting that a $4 billion program is creating perverse outcomes is portrayed as threatening the existence of the Plan itself. It seems we have a choice: either a Basin Plan, or good governance, accountability and transparency – but not both.

A binary debate suits the government. The Plan has seen a massive shift of wealth under the veil of environmental reform. Lifting the veil and questioning the reform risks highlighting that regions are suffering not because of the environment, but due to a failure of governments. Arguments about environment versus irrigation are a distraction from the lack of policies for regional economic development, agriculture or drought. The Plan has become the crowning achievement, an end in itself.

This is the post-truth water world that Quentin Grafton describes. If there is no space to discuss what is not working with the Plan, or the inefficient petrol combustion engine, how is it possible to upgrade it? Real problems are attributed to drought or ignorance. The recently released Keelty report echoes statements made by Phillip Glyde that people have either made bad business decisions or don't understand a key component of their business: water. Both are dog-whistling the idea of "stupid farmers." Stupid isn't the government's fault.

Perhaps the Basin's most sacred cow is the water market. When one questions the water market, the response is invariably along the lines of "You can't tell farmers what to grow," often followed up with a derisive reference to the Soviet Union. It seems there is only one possible policy response unless we embrace a failed communist model, even though governments didn't tell farmers what to grow before there was no market. I argue that the most commonly cited principle underlying the market – that water will flow to the "highest value use" – has failed us. Value was never defined, never debated. Water does not move to its highest value use for the community, the economy or even the country. It moves to whomever is prepared to pay the most: how many dollars can be made from a litre of water? If a dairy farmer or rice grower, for example, cannot make the same dollars per megalitre as an almond or cotton grower, they are condemned as less efficient, of less value. "Highest value use" is therefore better described as "greatest ability to pay."

There is no space in this system of "world's best practice" to value regional communities, "low-value" irrigators, Aboriginal people or the environment. Even after all these years, Aboriginal people and the environment are, in practice, external to the narrow concept of value that currently drives water management in the Basin. Some irrigators and their communities are now finding themselves in the same situation.

The "highest value use" argument relies on a functioning global food network. Currently, we use a great deal of our water to grow cotton and nuts, and export more than 90 per cent of them. Last year we imported more than 90 per cent of our rice, a third of our wheat on the east coast and half of our dairy products. COVID-19 threatens food supply and distribution. Vietnam, where most of our rice comes from, has stopped exporting it, and several other countries have followed suit. Shipping lanes are in disarray, making it difficult to get ships in or out. At the time of writing, it is possible we will have a rice and wheat (on the east coast) shortage for several months this year. We need to rethink our water and agricultural policies and consider other definitions of value. What does highest value use look like in a pandemic?

Irrigator Chris Brooks is trying to alert the public to the impending food shortages. He has called for the water that we do have to be made available for food. Brooks, and the people he represents, have been labelled as cynical opportunists selfishly exploiting the crisis. At a time when we are re-examining all aspects of our economy, we still cannot escape the binary narrative of greedy irrigator versus the environment that has dogged the public debate for more than a decade.

As a rebuttal to Brooks' warnings, Minister Littleproud, the National Farmers' Federation and the Authority have all alleged "scaremongering," claiming that Australia can feed 75 million people. The Australian Bureau of Agricultural and Resource Economics and Sciences hastily produced a report saying that Australia exports 70 per cent of its agricultural produce. Both statistics are misleading. They don't reveal that more than a third of those exports are cotton, wool and forest products, or that those statistics are based on our highest irrigation years and not the current drought.

The two bureaucrats who feature most often in the essay are the head of the Authority, Phillip Glyde, and the Commonwealth Environmental Water Holder, Jody Swirepik. They express frustration and dismay, and give an impression of powerlessness and fatigue. "We have to be in it for the long haul," "It's too soon, we have to be patient," "That's not our job." They look for signs of success at an ever-smaller level, while the grand endeavour is unravelling across the big, important measures, especially ecological health and community fairness.

If the architects and implementers of the Plan seem bemused at this unravelling, Glyde, at least, is clearly annoyed with Brooks for "jumping up and down" and getting in the way. Brooks is exercising his right in this democratic society to have his voice and the voice of his people heard. Unlike most, he has the means to do it.

At least once a month, and sometimes weekly, I will get a call from a stranger asking for help with water. Their stories all involve a severe impact on their livelihoods, families and sometimes their own sanity, over years and sometimes decades. There is always injustice, inequity and a shift of wealth. They have exhausted every avenue possible through politicians, three levels of government and their agencies and regulators. Mostly, they express disbelief that the government can do this to them, despite the inarguable evidence that it has.

In a recent Senate Estimates hearing, Glyde was asked about the fate of the Lower Darling irrigators, like Alan Whyte and Rachel Strachan. He explained that the Plan created "winners and losers." Presumably the people who ring me are among the losers. Unlike Brooks, they should accept their fate and go quietly.

Bureaucrats who have spent their lives in a system and are justifiably proud of their work almost always respond to the collapse or failure of that system by doing more of what got the system going in the first place – "do as before but more," in the words of C.S. Holling. Not only can they not do anything different, they can't *imagine* doing anything different. The voices of dissent, the voices of rural Australia, cannot be heard because they distract from the business of doing more of the same. As Simons points out, this will eventually play out in courts of law.

Simons' essay goes on to ask some critical questions: Can our current systems possibly meet the needs of the nation and the certainty of change? Is the Plan an honest compact, and is it fair? Can it work, and are our politics up to the task? And what happens when the macro policy, the plumbing, the schemes, the "events" or lack of them hit the realities of the landscape and the figures within it? After years of avoiding these questions, trying to answer them may be now be forced upon us.

The *Water Act* and the Basin Plan were well intentioned, but the Plan has been derailed by vested interests supported by the National Party. Important parts of the Plan aren't working because the system of which it is a part doesn't work. The Plan is a relic of a time and a system that no longer exists. Change will be forced upon us, probably by a changing climate and the changes to society it brings about. COVID-19 has brought into the present many things we thought we could put off.

If we want two irrigated monocultures in the Basin, hollowed-out regions and reliance on other countries for our food, then the water reforms are a success. If we want a diverse agricultural sector, vibrant communities and to grow what we eat, we need new water policies, as well as policies for regional economic development. To achieve this, we need to allow an honest and inclusive public debate and banish the binary rhetoric.

Maryanne Slattery

Correspondence

Mike Young

Margaret Simons' essay *Cry Me a River* came out a few weeks before the official report of the Interim Inspector-General for the Murray–Darling Basin, Mick Keelty: *Impact of Lower Inflows on State Shares under the Murray–Darling Basin Agreement*. Both are worth a careful read. Fascinated that Simons had got it so right, I read her essay in a single sitting. She documents superbly the depth of feeling and misunderstanding in the Basin, and how politicians have attempted to frustrate progress. As the American water administrator Tim Quinn has recently observed in California, "Too often, water policy leaders and stakeholders focus almost exclusively on *what should be done* rather than the *process for making those decisions*."

Throughout the millennium drought, Australia was committed to searching for excellence in water management. We had the process right. The search led to a total rewrite of water management legislation in all Basin states, the complete re-specification of our water rights system and the development of one of the world's best water-trading systems. The rest of the world was envious: by attending to basic concepts and agreeing to core principles, we were getting the detail right. However, the last decade has been characterised by compromise. To an outsider looking in, we have lost our way.

In 2006 and 2007, as the millennium drought deepened, it became obvious that we needed a better way to manage the Basin – something like an independent Reserve Bank for Water and a comprehensive plan. The proposed planning and water allocation system would need to cover groundwater as well as surface water, include powers to control overland flows and, as required under the National Water Initiative, bring an end to over-allocation. As Simons explains, all the leaders involved agreed. It was time for a rethink.

The legislation for a Basin-wide plan and an independent Murray–Darling Basin Authority emerged in 2008 and, while it still had a few gaps, it allowed Australia to claim, for a second time, the title of world's best water manager. But state ministers and water managers wanted to remain in control and, as Simons ably outlines, they jostled their way back to a position where they could prevent the emergence of an Authority that put Australia's collective interests first rather than their local interests.

Mick Keelty's report, which has been accepted by the federal government, points to a failure of those involved in Basin politics to get their heads around a host of basic water management concepts, and to a lack of leadership. Both are urgently required. The Basin lacks a person who is seen to be responsible for calling the shots and has the expertise to speak with authority and the insight to find the right solutions.

The primary role of leaders is to create a sense of trust in the process. So far, those involved have not been able to do this. Simons suggests that while all the efforts to frustrate progress and hijack agendas may be to the short-term benefit of some, they have come at a massive long-term cost to all. It is time for our leaders to stop supporting one solution over another and, instead, focus on fixing Basin governance: its legislation, policies and the Plan. The leaders must now commit to putting a state-of-the-art plan in place and make sure that everyone understands both what is required and why it is so important.

Simons and Keelty make another important point: in recent years the Basin has got much drier, as the figure on the following page, from Keelty's report, shows. For too long, water allocation plans have focused on the long-term average. A better approach, as Simons points out, would replace all arguments about volumes with a discussion of how to share water when it is wet and when it is dry, and how to put a strong water-sharing system in place. Robust water entitlement and allocation systems are designed to cope with long drys and even a permanently drier climate.

In the UK, water managers spend a lot of time working out how much water has to be left in each river to ensure the entire system remains healthy – all the way from its source to the sea. Innovatively, they call this water a "hands-off flow", and it is allocated first. No one is allowed to touch this water. Keelty devotes an entire chapter in his report to the Australian equivalent: conveyance water. The need to ensure that there is always enough water flowing to ensure the system's basic health is poorly understood. Conveyance water is an appropriate name for the Southern Connected Basin, but for the Darling system I prefer the UK term, as it so powerfully gets the message across. Some water always has to be left in the system. In retrospect, it is obvious that all involved have spent way too much time arguing over maximum amounts that can be taken and not nearly enough about minimum flows.

Keelty's explanation of how much drier it has been in the past twenty years, with the water necessary for conveyance superimposed on top (Southern Connected Murray River System only).

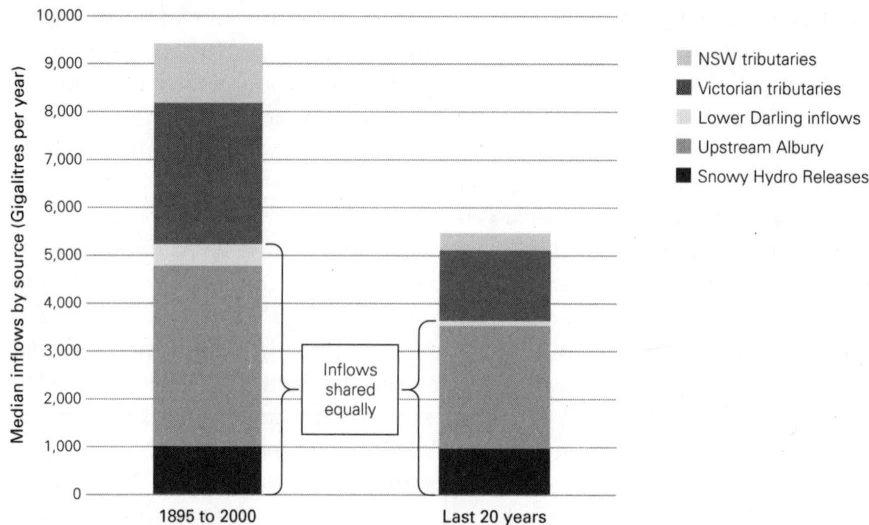

A properly designed system would start by putting aside enough water for conveyance and deciding how to share access to the remainder. These are difficult decisions, as they involve risks and trade-offs. Try deducting 2000 gigalitres from the bottom of the above graph and then working out how much the water available to be "used" has declined. The answer is quite frightening. Small declines in rainfall mean much larger declines in the amount of water flowing into the river and much, much less water that can be used. As a rule of thumb, a 10 per cent decline in mean rainfall can result in a 30 to 40 per cent decline in inflows and, as the base flow still needs to be maintained, as much as a 60 or 70 per cent decline in the amount that can be taken out of the system and used for irrigation, discretionary environmental objectives, etc.

Recognising the importance of this basic concept, at the end of her essay Simons reports a sad but illuminating "water-sharing" discussion with the Authority's current CEO, Phillip Glyde. Sitting down with Glyde, she raises the need for a dynamic sharing system – one that would adjust automatically to changes in the health of the system and recent inflows. Glyde agrees that such a system is required.

No argument. But then he goes on to explain that during the development of the Basin Plan, rather than requiring a robust water-sharing system, it was decided to set sustainable diversion limits for each part of the Basin and define them as a fixed number. SDLs, as they are called up and down the Basin, "were required for legal reasons and also 'for bringing people along reasons.'" Tellingly, Glyde then goes on to say that "perhaps in twenty or thirty years, 'in Basin Plan Mark Four or Five,'" such a system could be put in place. When the CEO – known for his pragmatism – thinks it will take three or more Plans to get the basics right, something is seriously wrong.

In closing, Simons observes that, "The political obstacles, the hate, the unfairness and the potentially catastrophic gaps in our knowledge obscure what an achievement it would be for the Murray–Darling Basin Plan to succeed." But what would it take to succeed? It would have to start with sensible amendments to the *Water Act*, followed by amendments to the raft of state and territory *Water Acts* that enable allocations to be made and then to each of the Basin's eighty or so local water-resource plans. This is a big job, but one worth doing. As Keelty also observes, there is an urgent need to improve water literacy, for a new apolitical leader and for much better engagement and consultation processes.

I hope we will see this include a much better understanding of the role of groundwater, the difference between gross and net water accounting systems, and the need to specify entitlements. Long ago, it was recognised that the Darling's water licensing system needed to be modified so that environmental water can be shepherded safely from one part of the Darling to another. As millions of dead fish are telling us, it is time to make it easy to shepherd (hands-off water) through the system. Simons includes many references to the importance of groundwater, including return flows. Sadly, however, those who drafted Keelty's terms of reference left out any requirement to consider groundwater. There is only one mention of it in his entire report.

Even more importantly, it is time for our political leaders to put Basin politics to one side, appoint a truly independent chair of the Authority and instruct this person to start searching for a suite of institutional and administrative arrangements that will serve those who live in the Basin, those who use its water resources and those who benefit from their existence. More than anything, the Basin needs a leader capable of restoring trust and developing a state-of-the-art solution rather than a messily negotiated suite of compromises.

Mike Young

CRY ME
A RIVER

Correspondence

Stuart Bunn

After several years of drought, tensions over water sharing have intensified, pitting environmental groups against farmers, north against south, with many stakeholders more upset with the government plan to fix the problem than the drought itself. Farmers are calling it a "man-made drought," complaining that water needed for crops is going to fish instead and that any that is allowed to flow to the ocean is wasted. Much of the water is now diverted upstream to fuel agricultural production on over a million hectares of farmland. But it is also needed to sustain the lower estuary and its wildlife, including several species listed as endangered and federally protected. The board responsible for water management strives to balance these and other environmental obligations with the needs of farmers – and no one is happy with the result. Compounding matters is the growing recognition that conditions are likely to become drier in the future and the acknowledgment that all sides will have to give up something.

The setting in question is the Sacramento–San Joaquin Delta, a key battleground in California's water wars – but it will no doubt resonate with those familiar with the challenges of the Murray–Darling Basin. Similar stories abound for rivers around the world, where growing demand has increased competition among water users (including the environment), and especially in regions such as California and southern Australia, which face a hotter, drier and more variable climate. Overlaying these biophysical constraints are the complicated institutional arrangements that enable sharing water across political boundaries.

Social concerns about the declining health of freshwater ecosystems and the associated loss of the essential services they provide are growing and are well justified. Globally, there is little evidence that we will meet the United Nations' Sustainable Development Goal 6.6: to "protect and restore water-related ecosystems." Wetlands are vanishing three times faster than forests, and freshwater biodiversity is declining at more than twice the rate observed in terrestrial or marine ecosystems. Continued decline in water quality and ecological health in the Murray–Darling Basin during the 1990s and the millennium drought were a catalyst for significant water reforms in Australia, especially the recovery of water for the environment. There was political and social consensus that the health of this critical asset was in peril.

Steve Posselt travelled the length of the Murray–Darling by kayak (by necessity, with wheels) in 2007 at the height of the millennium drought to highlight the plight of the river in his book *Cry Me a River*. Margaret Simons' essay of the same name takes us on a very different journey. Drawing on a broad range of interviews and discussions, including with landowners, bureaucrats and academics, her story seems to have the elements of a good tragedy – a tragic hero (the river) cursed by fate and a fatal flaw (not enough water), the struggle between good and evil, and the sense of tragic waste as the hero meets his logical destruction in the final act, with things working out poorly for everyone.

Simons highlights the challenges faced by Basin communities, the environment and those charged with managing the system. She acknowledges the difficulty of negotiating a new sustainable diversion limit to meet the primary goal of the 2007 *Water Act*, to "protect, restore and provide for the ecological values of ecosystems." But despite this, she devotes little attention to the good work being undertaken by the Commonwealth Environmental Water Office or to the perspectives of ecologists concerned for the health of the river.

Simons' essay provides insight into the complicated arrangements for water sharing among the states and the ongoing efforts to maintain the political compact that is the Basin Plan. Above all, the essay conveys a sense of hopeless struggle to understand the complexities of water management and to reach agreement on how best to share the water at a Basin-wide scale. However, it stops short of finding workable solutions to these wicked problems.

Sustainable water management is fiendishly complex. Although the woes of the Basin are often in the news, Australia has earned a strong reputation overseas for its approach to water management. The 2007 *Water Act* ensures the Basin is managed in the national interest, building on nearly 100 years of reform since the first River Murray Water Agreement was signed. Getting the states to agree to a whole-of-Basin plan that addresses competing state interests and rebalances the share with the environment was no small achievement. Other countries acknowledge this: indeed many, including the United States, India, Brazil and China, have looked to Australia for lessons that can be learnt.

The Plan must ensure decisions are made in the national interest. One of the key challenges in reaching a common perspective – highlighted by Simons – is that "everyone downstream is a wastrel, and everyone upstream is a thief. Only I, the person drawing water in this spot, for these crops, in this way, truly understands the value of the water and how to use it." Although we speak of the "Basin community," as Simons notes, they don't act as one because they struggle to recognise a common interest.

The Basin Plan sets a new sustainable diversion limit: the amount of water that can be taken from the river system for consumptive purposes. The final amount of water to be recovered was agreed as part of the political settlement and is less than the initial estimates informed by science. Significantly, most of the water for the environment has already been recovered and all water recovery has been voluntary – either purchased direct, or as an outcome of investments in irrigation efficiency. We know this adjustment has not been without its impacts. Many small rural communities are feeling the loss of the water and require additional support.

Although Basin communities have struggled with the rapid pace of reform, the Plan does take a long-term perspective. We've always maintained it was a starting point and adjustments would be needed in both the short and long term. The evaluation of the Basin Plan in 2026 allows for larger adjustments, but smaller ones can be made before then. For example, water resource plans set out how the states will adhere to the new sustainable diversion limits and were meant to be in place by mid-2019. Some of these plans have been delayed and there have been allowances made to give states more time to complete them.

New information is emerging as the NSW government undertakes its Healthy Floodplains project, which aims to reform the management of floodplain harvesting through licensing, monitoring and regulation. This new information will be built into the Plan.

Climate change poses a massive challenge for the Basin and will undoubtedly require a revisit of the broader settings of the Plan, with new data revealing that inflows in the Southern Basin have almost halved in the past twenty years. The irrigation industry, rural communities and the environment are all going to have to adapt and make the transition to a quite different – likely hotter, drier and more variable – climate. The Basin Plan doesn't end in 2026 and will be a blueprint for the way ahead. Drought, bushfires and pandemics make this job tougher, but there is no Plan B.

Although the Authority has the role of river operator on behalf of the southern states, its primary role under the *Water Act* is to oversee and regulate water use within the Basin. This is a stewardship role that requires the states to stay the course and remain committed to the Plan. With six governments and seven houses of parliament across the Basin, maintaining productive relationships among the parties is of paramount importance.

We agree fully with Margaret Simons' finding of the importance of rebuilding trust – we acknowledge that is no easy task. It is multifaceted and requires the effort and commitment of all governments. It means greater transparency in reporting, clearer and more open communication and engagement with communities, and a genuine promise to embrace opportunities to adjust and adapt.

We are determined to call out any backsliding from these commitments. We will ensure water resource and water-sharing plans are consistent with the Basin Plan, and that there is full recovery of water. We are strengthening our compliance program and ensuring that water users are doing what they are meant to do so the community can have more confidence.

We will continue on our path of regionalisation. By mid-2021, one-third of our workforce will be dispersed in the Basin region. This is our commitment to building stronger working relationships with Basin communities.

Eight years in, we've made good progress implementing the Plan – a difficult but necessary reform. We can't lose sight of the achievements. Around 2100 gigalitres of water have been recovered for the environment and there are early signs of improvement in river health. But we still have some way to go.

The Plan offers our best hope for a transparent and fair approach to managing the water resources of the Basin in a more sustainable way. We will only achieve that if all parties involved stay the course and adjust and improve their operations within the agreed framework of the Plan. The story of the Murray–Darling doesn't have to be a tragedy.

Stuart Bunn

CRY ME A RIVER

Correspondence

Gabrielle Chan

When Margaret Simons set out to write her essay on the Murray–Darling Basin, she didn't know it would crash headlong into a global pandemic. Just as her essay was released, COVID-19 sparked panic-buying in supermarkets. Australians were confronted by a shortage of toilet paper and basic food stuffs: staples such as mince, flour and pasta. Fruit and vegetable prices went up. I paid $11 for a cauliflower.

The empty shelves were a result of distribution issues, with one exception: Australian rice production has been devastated by drought and water allocations, and countries such as Vietnam have halted exports to protect their own food security. But apart from rice, we discovered that a global supply chain that provides goods "just in time" does not work well when consumer behaviour changes suddenly.

The shortages sparked a debate about food security. Some Southern Basin irrigators urged the government to release more water to grow staples like rice, which are not as profitable as horticulture or permanent nut trees. But the National Farmers' Federation said food security was the one thing Australians don't have to worry about, and the Australian Bureau of Agricultural and Resource Economics (ABARES) released a document that concluded "Australia does not have a food security problem."

With Australian water trading privileging the highest economic return, we have given priority to profit over value – a questionable assumption in the case of both human sustenance and the health of the natural world. Nuts good, milk and rice bad. That is the ruthless equation of the market. The ABARES report said government intervention would provide, among other things, "water that would have been used more profitably in another sector (reducing the gross value of irrigated production)." This is the natural endpoint of valuing water as if it were widgets. Values and food diversity cannot trump profits.

Yet governments intervene all the time. The pandemic drama occurred after a specific lack of water (drought) in the Basin (although there have since been falls of rain that may presage a good season for eastern-state food producers). Three years of lack of water has seen the government claim to have spent $7 billion on drought because it values farmers.

All of these issues were in the back of my mind when I read *Cry Me a River*. It is quite simply the clearest, fairest picture of the very complex Basin system I have read. And being clear and fair is important in this debate, because the intricacies of the stressed natural system, fracturing local communities and shocking politics obstruct the path to a good result for the whole country. Some politicians, lobbyists, irrigators and environmentalists deliberately use the complexities of the system and its often incomprehensible language to obscure the debate and their part in it. Politicians have said as much when they are threatened with media scrutiny. They know any journalist trying to shine a spotlight on the issue will quickly run out of time, knowledge or puff. The dogs bark and the caravan moves on, as Keating once said.

If you are new to river reading and it's all a mess of stupefying terms and confusing counter-claims, these are the perverse points that crystallised for me from Simons' essay.

First, the river will never return to a completely natural state. Even the Commonwealth Environmental Water Holder, Jody Swirepik, acknowledges that "we are not trying to change things back to natural. That's not possible."

Second, with the exception of "the water thieves and possibly corrupt politicians and bureaucrats" – pending ICAC investigations – everyone has done what they have been allowed to do by governments and policy-makers. People are like water; their operations will flow through any gaps permitted by the system. It is the job of state and federal governments to design a system that does not allow economic, environmental and social perversity.

Third, there needs to be some transparency. It is possible for ordinary citizens to find out who owns shares and real estate. It is not possible to uncover how much water is in the Basin system and how much is owned. Conspiracy theories, real and imagined, will continue until this is fixed.

Fourth, water efficiency infrastructure paid for in billions by the taxpayer has increased water take, because the changes have eliminated "return flows" to the environment. By replacing the leaky pivot and the canal used by birds, animals and insects, we have effectively cut off a proportion of water supply to natural environments throughout the Basin. This means a chunk of environmental water savings has been cancelled out at great cost to nature and the taxpayer.

Fifth, Australia can't start again on another plan. It must fix the existing one, which has already cleared the first hurdle of tying the states and the Commonwealth together. So reform must begin from here. Australians cannot let the protagonists walk off in a huff. Otherwise, foundational reforms designed to return water to the environment and bring certainty to communities will do neither.

The chorus of criticism is loud. Communities in the Southern Basin that have long been politically stable are now – with some success – organising candidates as a reaction against current water management. Two NSW Nationals MPs lost their seats over water in the 2019 state election, and the current environment minister, Sussan Ley, got a fright in the federal election two months later.

Scientists have been scathing. The Wentworth Group's submission to the South Australian royal commission did not miss. "Serious management failures have eroded the public trust in governments to successfully implement reforms. Without major changes in implementation, it is almost certain that the Basin Plan will fail."

The Productivity Commission's five-year assessment in 2019 was pessimistic about the road ahead. "In the Commission's view, the significant risks to implementation cannot be managed effectively under current institutional and governance arrangements. Reform is required." Why? Because the river system is so important to the eastern-state landscapes, our domestic food supply, our export industries and the natural capital that powers our society.

The only thing I felt Simons' essay lacked was a shortlist of potential reforms going forward, distilled from the forty or so reviews and reports into the Basin. (Which is not a criticism so much as a wish – her job was hard enough.) Such a list might help governments plug the holes in water management, and they do need simplicity in order to focus in desperate times.

So let me nominate two by way of example. The first is transparency. In April 2020, former Australian Federal Police commissioner Mick Keelty's report into the Basin was released, urging government to set up a "single point of truth." An open water register for all to see, including the water holdings of politicians, would silence the rumour mill and identify the dogs in the race. We could see clearly how much water there is, who owns it and where it is going.

The second is carving up the Murray–Darling Basin Authority, which has the dual roles of trying to keep the Plan on the rails and overseeing compliance. The Productivity Commission pointed out that these roles are often in conflict. That would only worsen in the next five years, the report said, and it recommended the Authority be split. Nothing has been done.

These sorts of reforms could be nutted out over the table of a future national cabinet, now that the COVID-19 crisis has pushed our governments to cooperate more effectively. "History suggests," Simons writes, "that it is only when there is a visible crisis that progress is made on managing the river." Winston Churchill said, "Never let a good crisis go to waste." Public debate around the Murray–Darling often comes down to binaries. People versus environment. Top-down policies devised by boffins versus bottom-up ones devised by communities. Letting big business rip in the water markets versus protecting small farmers. None of this serves the country. Humans are part of the environment. Experts can produce policy while communities can take the unintended edges off. Diversity of businesses provides stability and fairness in the production of food. If we are capable of locking down for months for a virus, surely we are capable of creating a plan to future-proof our food, our natural world and the people who live in it.

Gabrielle Chan

Correspondence

Geoff Beeson

My most recent trip along the Darling River, from Wentworth to Brewarrina and beyond, was in late October 2019, just a short time before Margaret Simons' own journey. I can readily confirm her reports of the resigned and frustrated attitudes of people in the river communities.

The chequered history of the development of the Basin Plan can be written in different ways. For those of us who were interested at the time, both the battle to get a supportable and workable plan and the intense criticisms over water allocations are hard to forget. I thought the tone of Simons' comments in places seemed at odds with the significance and complexity of the plan and the fact that a major landmark reform ultimately achieved approval in both houses of parliament, despite the government not having a majority in the Senate. An example is her observation that the government of the day "apparently had no strategy to deal with the political consequences – other than to crumble." At the time, there were many – including me – who urged the minister to seek a more ambitious target for environmental water recovery. However, there is a strong likelihood that such a target would not have been approved by the Senate, as Simons acknowledges. While the Plan approved by the parliament was not ideal from many points of view, it was major reform in a conflicted area, to which federal and relevant state and territory governments committed, and it received international recognition. Where it is now failing is in its implementation.

Simons has rightly identified a terrible array of obstacles that together constitute an almost insurmountable hurdle to successful implementation of the Plan. On top of this, she argues that "the politics have become close to unmanageable." It is hard to disagree. However, despite this, a way forward must be found. The Basin Plan is too important to fail. The problems caused by the over-allocation of water and the continued threat of increasing water scarcity will not go away by themselves.

We should address three fundamental and interrelated factors if we are to make progress: context, status and leadership.

Context

A serious weakness of the current approach is that the Murray–Darling Basin Plan is treated in isolation. It sits out on its own, rather than being framed as part of one of the great challenges facing our country: water security. In the driest inhabited continent on the planet, to ensure a reliable and sufficient supply of water of suitable quality everywhere it is needed will always be an issue. At present, water scarcity in Australia is increasing, due to decreased rainfall in some parts of the country, including the south-east; increasing population; and greater demands for water for agriculture. Climate change is making the situation worse. Capital cities and many inland towns and cities have been forced to introduce water restrictions in recent years, and seawater desalination plants have been built in five of the capital cities. In some inland towns and farms, water has had to be trucked in. The south-west of the continent, including the Western Australian grain belt, has experienced decades of drying, to a far greater extent than was predicted in the 1980s. As occurs in all droughts, the recent drought in eastern Australia, especially in New South Wales, has intensified the difficulties and hardships of seasonal dry periods.

Important initiatives have been made and are continuing to be made in water conservation, the use of recycled water and stormwater, using aquifers for storage and later recovery, increasing productivity of the available water, and in water-efficient design. These methods have been used variously in towns, cities, farming communities and specifically in irrigation, including the transport of water and its application to crops. Before it was abolished in 2014, the National Water Commission performed a valuable role in this area, including supporting the use of recycled water and making strategic investments in managed aquifer recharge. It also had the role of auditing the implementation of the Basin Plan.

The point here is that the pressing need to redress over-allocation of water in the Murray–Darling Basin must surely be seen as part of the broader imperative to ensure reliable water supplies to all communities for personal, domestic, commercial, industrial, agricultural and recreational needs. Also in this mix should be a national strategy to deal with the periodic droughts which inevitably occur, rather than taking panic actions when these droughts are upon us. Viewing the issue this way would encourage more coherent policy development, and help those outside the Basin, specifically city dwellers, to better understand the significance of the Murray–Darling Basin Plan.

Status

Water and how it is managed is a high national priority. Ensuring the long-term sustainability of the Murray–Darling Basin is a nation-building project, especially given the Basin's centrality in food and fibre production and its contribution to the nation's economy. It easily ranks in importance with other, more readily recognised nation-building projects, such as the Sydney Harbour Bridge, the Overland Telegraph Line, the Kiewa Hydro-Electric Scheme or even modern-day road or rail projects. Yet it does not appear to have this status in the wider community or in official circles. It is not recorded on lists of major infrastructure projects, nor is it referred to as a nation-building project in discussions about the Basin. It appears as a poor cousin to other significant projects, and mostly as a source of inter-region, inter-state and state–federal conflicts, the reasons for which are too complex for all but specialist professionals to comprehend. This lowly status works against recognition of its significance to the wider community, and consequently against effective accountability for actions taken and resources expended. It also misses out on the psychological value in recognising it as a nation-building project.

Leadership

Past successful Australian nation-building projects have been supported by strong leadership from state or federal governments, or, in the case of multi-state projects, both – and sometimes from an individual champion as well (for example, J.J.C. Bradfield for the Sydney Harbour Bridge). This key feature has been missing from the implementation of the Basin Plan for several years. In fact, the federal Coalition government has been backing away from the Plan since 2014. It has given priority to infrastructure developments over much cheaper water buybacks, lowered the target for environmental water recovery, provided lax oversight of water-trading rules, and cast doubt on the feasibility of achieving additional savings of 450 gigalitres, to which all parties had previously agreed. The government has consistently ignored the recommendations of credible independent bodies – the Productivity Commission, the South Australian royal commission, the Australian Academy of Science – despite a strong level of agreement in their major recommendations. An independent review in 2017 found that some states, especially New South Wales and Queensland, showed an alarmingly low level of compliance with the Plan when it came to water extraction, and a conspicuous lack of transparency. As Simons records, New South Wales also makes regular threats to withdraw from the Plan, despite having committed to it in 2012.

Normally, we might expect the necessary national leadership to come from the relevant minister in the federal government, but this too has been lacking in recent years. As Simons illustrates, leadership has been abdicated in favour of side deals to satisfy sectional interests. In a telling move, responsibility for water policy and resources was shifted from the Department of the Environment to the Department of Agriculture in 2015. In a further change, in February 2020 a new combined department with three ministers came into being: the Department of Agriculture, Water and the Environment. To whom might we now look for the crucial leadership of the Murray–Darling Basin Plan? The Minister for Agriculture, Drought and Emergency Management (presumably the senior minister)? The Minister for the Environment? Or the Minister for Resources, Water and Northern Australia? Water security issues are involved in all three ministries.

Somehow out of this confusion of responsibilities, strong leadership for implementing the Basin Plan must emerge. One of the factors that makes the Murray–Darling Basin policy so problematic is that consistent commitment at the state level is also crucial. However, the whole policy must be led at the national level, so the federal government is the place to start. There are examples of successful large-scale agricultural and environmental reforms involving cooperation between federal and state governments. Simons mentions the management of salinity in the 1980s and '90s. Another is the Great Artesian Basin Sustainability Initiative, which involved capping hundreds of uncontrolled artesian bores, replacing thousands of kilometres of open earthen drains and establishing a basin-wide monitoring and information network. It stopped decades of waste of valuable water and widespread environmental degradation, and brought major benefits for the landholders involved.

If these three issues are resolved – a broader focus on water, ensuring it has a high status in the Australian community, and strong and unwavering leadership – other urgent matters can then be addressed. These include: a pause on so-called efficiency projects, a comprehensive water audit, a plan for the collaborative involvement of affected communities, a plan to ensure the water market works effectively, and a transparent monitoring and evaluation regime that promotes continual improvement. Effective use of expert advice would be an essential part of this. We should also hope that, with more coherent policies, counter-productive steps such as the abolition of the National Water Commission would not be taken.

Without these actions, it is almost certain the Murray–Darling Basin Plan will fail. If it does, the $13 billion committed by Australian taxpayers will be largely wasted. Many of our rivers, such as the Darling, along with their communities, will die. The future for many in the Basin will be uncertain, and we will pass this uncertainty on to future generations, along with a degraded environment. What government would allow itself to be responsible for this? We cannot let it happen.

Geoff Beeson

Barney Foran

What an affair of the heart Margaret Simons' *Cry Me a River* offers the weary water watcher. Several things struck me on reading this stupendous essay. Indigenous understanding and narratives reminded me how "pump and drain" our management has become. We hide behind spreadsheets and models, buffered by our leafy suburbs and café culture. And what a trip Margaret had, driving the dusty, corrugated roads while sniffing along a river reach for an insight. I grin when I think of the pub sessions, the reticence on the first beer and then the flood of indictments on the fifth or sixth, and those "million-mile stares" when interviewees considered climate change. Finally, I found myself acknowledging the positions of most interviewees, whether they were up to their armpits in dead fish or politically nuancing a fine policy point in a Canberra bureau.

Given a century of chaos and politicking, it's understandable that *Cry Me a River* does not end with a neat five points for action. Rather, Simons appeals to us to find a way through, as time is running short:

> The political obstacles, the hate, the unfairness and the potentially catastrophic gaps in our knowledge obscure what an achievement it would be for the Murray–Darling Basin Plan to succeed. A voluntary scheme to peg back use of an overstretched resource would be close to unprecedented in the world. Perhaps, in the face of the evidence, it might mean there is hope for our system of governance, for our politics, and for us all.

I was never part of the "water wars," but I worked in a CSIRO group that brought together all the physical bits that make the Australian economy tick (the physical economy) and crafted it into a coherent analytical framework to aid consideration of big policy questions such as human population, marine fisheries, energy and greenhouse, and land and water. This gave us the helicopter or million-square-kilometre view. We ended up in all sorts of policy strife when today's settings were kicked down the road to 2050 or so. Many of my close colleagues were deep in the fight, being told their attitudes were "career-ending," as they argued through the big numbers required to regain the function and fluency of the Basin. I remember returning to a head-office storm in Canberra after I spoke to a Queensland parliamentary committee during a drought and proposed we all pay a cappuccino tax of fifty cents per cup to bolster the struggling dairy industry and share the pain.

"Why is this all so hard?" we ask, as we read Simons' essay. Part of the explanation lies in economic theory. When quants discuss policy shocks to the economic system, they assume that production is a function of capital and labour. The 1987 Nobel laureate Robert Solow explored this in the mid-1950s, finding there was a sizeable lump (the so-called Solow residual) left over after labour and capital; this is now called "multi-factor productivity" or "how bright and innovative we are." When two physicists, German Reiner Kummel and American Robert Ayres, got hold of the problem, they found that energy use explained all of the Solow residual. In other words, the physical world is central to economic production. Failure to acknowledge this underpins the intractability, anger and water theft reported throughout the essay. Thus, to run the numbers properly, productivity must be a function of capital, labour, energy and materials (p = k,l,e,m), water being a material central to production. The dissonance Simons' essay describes in water policy (and equally, federal energy policy) is because these physical determinants of production are not accepted fully within ideology or analysis. Today's water prices better value the scarce water resource and, as Simons details, water is sent to almond growers, leaving rice growers high and dry. But as with the electricity market, spot dollar prices alone do not keep the river flowing or the lights on. Until we broaden the value equation, there will be no peace in the Basin.

Cry Me a River necessarily deals in big numbers: gigalitres (GL or one billion litres), which contain many Olympic swimming pools; and my favourite – Sydney Harbour Equivalents, or SYDARBs. So now for a few more important terms. Simons' essay focuses on "blue water," the stuff in dams, aquifers and getting choked in the Barmah Choke. Equally important is "green water," the stuff stored in the soil where we grow our grains and pasture our animals. There is also "white water," the stuff in air transpired by plants. Clearing the bush over the last 220 years for crops and pastures resulted in a lot of big shifts between these buckets, and "green water" will now be critical to the future of the Basin. Continent-wide land-clearing reduced water transpired by native vegetation (white water) by 340,000 gigalitres, roughly fifteen times the amount of blue water we manage nationally, a seismic alteration we've been trying to band-aid over ever since. Given the halving of inflows to the Basin reported by Mick Keelty's review, radically revamping on-farm custody of green water is an even bigger challenge than the blue water chaos Simons details. Charles Massey's *Call of the Reed Warbler* describes the efforts of regenerative farmers to implement a modern agriculture based on soil structure, water-holding capacity and nutrient cycling. Parsimony in blue and green water management will dictate the Basin's ability to feed, clothe and help balance trade in the twenty-first century.

Then there is "virtual water." The Basin exports water embodied in goods and services, and the nation imports it as well. Nationally, one year's analysis showed that we exported 7500 gigalitres' worth of "blue water" and imported 3500 gigalitres, a net loss of 4000 gigalitres. Mostly commentators would consider this acceptable and would note "competitive and comparative advantage," "we help feed the world" and so on. The 4000-gigalitre trade deficit is an interesting bucket, considering it is the same amount many river ecologists agree is needed to restore the Basin to ecological health.

Now for some more terminology used in water accounting: "scarce water flows," water traded in our "dry water economy." Scarce water is much the same as the untouched baseflows which, as Simons relates, Mike Young tried to get Minister Turnbull to include in the *Water Act* and was told, "Mike ... you are no longer being useful." Australia is among the top ten exporters of scarce water internationally, joining countries such as India, Pakistan, Syria, Egypt and Turkmenistan. Top scarce water importers include Japan, Germany, the United States, the UK and France, who use trade advantage and established production chains, some from colonial times, to acquire their needs. The reckoning here is not just that we export scarce water, but whether we get appropriate financial and social returns from doing so. *Cry Me a River* argues unequivocally that we do not.

Virtual water, the sum total of blue water embodied in the global production chain, can be used for good (measuring, monitoring and improving) or as a means of abuse (attacks on commodities and industries). A cursory Google search tells us 1 kilo of beef on a plate requires 20,000 litres of virtual water or more. Therefore, doing without 1 kilo of beef allows you to shower guilt-free for a year. However, forensic accounting of beef farms in Australia and New Zealand produces a figure of between 20 and 500 litres per kilogram of beef on the plate, depending on the production system. Green water (soil water from rainfall) should be excluded and blue water alone included in such accounting. Irrigated forage, whether in field or for feedlot, increases the virtual water content and so provides consumers with the timely, quality product we demand. So too for milk production, which can vary from 50 to 1000 litres of blue water per litre, depending on the amount of irrigation, grain and concentrate used in the production system.

And so to the perceived problem of cotton – regional development king, international trade darling and water harvester of the northern flows. Top cotton farmers use around 3000 litres of water per kilogram of cotton lint for spinning. The untold story is cottonseed, over half by weight of the big round bales you see in the field. Cottonseed oil gets high marks for the deep-frying of Friday fish and chips, while the high-protein cottonseed cake remainder underpins animal production chains in poultry, pork, beef and dairy. The Basin's cotton producers and water activists need to acknowledge this production mix and its advantages more fully. So too the Australian consumer, who needs to understand better where food and clothing come from. The chance to spin and weave Australian cotton locally was unfortunately another missed opportunity. Industry leaders tried to interest Australian banks in a high-tech robotic plant that would equal the production capacities and prices of our low-wage Asian neighbours, where our cotton is processed now. Sadly, our banks backed the IT frenzy of the time and now Basin water provides few downstream jobs in domestic cotton production.

In *Cry Me a River*, Simons impressed me with the technical accuracy of her succinct and fluent explanations. Navigating the conflicting analyses of the bottom lakes was deftly done. Taking on the concept of water-use efficiency and "water rebound" – the work of John Williams and Quentin Grafton – requires wide exposure to the policy world, where efficiency and growth are the mantras of our times. Who would believe that implementing efficiency would actually give less water flow, and that a billion-dollar efficiency investment was yet another industry subsidy at a time of water crisis? Initially it is hard to accept that replacing flood irrigation with centre pivot giants and drip-lines gives bad river outcomes for an over-used basin. But it's obvious when you think about it: water applied just to the cropping rootzone allows little to seep away and so maintain the river downstream.

Given the unruly and competing interests that Simons presents, it is inevitable that she avoids indicating how Australian consumers and citizens might moderate her "cry" to an occasional whimper. The response to COVID-19 will result in the retreat of extreme globalisation and changes in our consumer mindset, so what can we do about water and the Basin? Below are some suggestions:

- Buy Australian wherever possible and look for the label stating how much of the product is home-grown. Get to know the growers and food processors who advertise how they are improving water and nutrient management. The Ricegrowers' Association of Australia is a good place to start.

- Leave one-dollar-a-litre milk and similar products on the shelf. This market furphy is sending milk growers broke and vastly undervalues the real value of water and the services required to better manage the Basin.
- Own fewer cotton clothes and wear them until they fall apart on you. I'd love to tell you all about Australian value-adding in weaving and garment manufacture, but apart from a weaver or two of organic and recycled cotton and some R.M. Williams classic lines, it's a thin story.
- Vegies, fruit and dairy staples always pose a problem for the water frugalist, as they require around 1000 litres per kilogram of product, more for concentrates like butter and cheese. So eat according to the health guidelines, avoid food waste and, if you can, grow some leafy greens with tank water.
- If you eat red meat, purchase grass-fed beef and lamb. This avoids hand-wringing about industrial feedlots, and fodder crops are grown with green water from rainfall rather than blue water. The white meats, chicken and pork, have a lower impact, but high-protein concentrates in feeds that might be dryland grown or irrigated can be an issue – producers should publish their production mix.
- Pasta is more water-frugal than rice if grain comes from dryland agriculture. But this should not diminish Australian rice, which has developed good environmental credentials.
- For almond milk consumers there is some difficult news. A 2018 peer-reviewed life cycle analysis shows it has the highest environmental impact across all categories (including embodied water), five times that of soy milk and twice that of cow milk.
- Finally, to the Friday night tipple, where beer mostly wins. This is usually made with rain-grown barley and irrigated hops, plus process water. Irrigated wine is much like irrigated milk and fruit juices, at 1000 litres per litre of product. Consider rain-grown wine; it is more expensive, so pay more, drink less.

Cry Me a River never flags. Simons writes with literary assurance, untangling complexity as she goes. She punches through the facts, figures, character assassinations and war stories, but then calms you with a place, a person and a rounded thought. This is writing of the highest calibre.

Barney Foran

CRY ME A RIVER

Correspondence

Lauren Rickards

In the early years of the millennium drought I worked as an in-house consultant to the Murray–Darling Basin Commission (now the Murray–Darling Basin Authority). In this role I developed a strong sense of the double reality Margaret Simons describes at the heart of the Basin planning woes. The MDBC corporate services sat at the top of the building. Up there, water existed only as a faint scent among the spreadsheets and carefully worded communications. It was a tense world, dominated by suits, ministerial demands, meeting agendas, whispers and double talk. Our job was to help hold together the fragile inter-state agreements needed to maintain the Basin's fragile flows.

On the lower floors of the building was another world, still within the MDBC but full of muddy boots, posters, maps and plants. During lunchtime runs up Mount Ainslie, I got to know some of the ecologists, hydrologists and others involved. Seemingly always dressed for field work, they had a palpable passion for water and rivers, for their work on streams and threatened species here, and local communities and fish traps there. Rather than the dry legal documents I had to wrangle upstairs, their work was about lively watery places, and the plants, animals and people inhabiting them. Yet it was also pervaded by a sense of frustration and even futility. They pumped me for detail on the decision-making upstairs to try to understand why their work seemed to be blown one way, then another. It was clear to all of us that their scientific research was not only inherently difficult, but also prone to misuse and neglect. It was not long before I quit.

Simons' story of her road trip around the Basin sharply illuminates the schism between the high-level governance of the Basin and the intimate details and messy complexities of actual places. But this is not a simple government-knocking tale. Simons' essay carefully illuminates many of the "horizontal" schisms that also characterise Basin planning, notably those between groups distinguished by location, identity and their interest in water. High-level, national policies like the Basin Plan are needed because of the fierce and often unfair competition among different water users, including those barely recognised as legitimate users, namely traditional owners and ecosystems. While the high-level view can callously ignore the anguish of local communities and the destruction of unique places, it can also reveal critical longer-term and larger-scale patterns that are often imperceptible or unpalatable to those on the ground. This perspective is vital to ensuring that the interests of the public and of marginalised groups are protected against brash and powerful commercial interests. The pressing need for environmental flows, to maintain the health of the river system and the myriad communities that rely on it, is one such pattern.

Simons highlights the way advocates for (and against) environmental flows often wrestle with the question of what is natural. The fraught notion of a "natural baseline" is always on the verge of collapsing under the weight of the rivers' variability and the effort of pretending that the world is static and the continent was empty before settlers. On the other hand, the natural baseline is a badly named but pragmatic tool for addressing the grim reality of a critically over-exploited system.

To my mind, the problem is not that the system designed to generate environmental flows utilises the idea of a natural baseline, but that it is based on a narrow, capitalist notion of "unused" resources as waste. In the coal and coal seam gas basins with which many water basins – including the Murray–Darling Basin – are entwined, the resource being "wasted" is coal or gas "left sitting underground," as if it has been caught idle. In water basins, the waste in question is water "left just flowing" through natural systems, whether in rivers, lakes or underground. As Simons notes, many Northern Basin irrigators see "water sent to the sea as 'waste'." Efforts to recover water for Murray–Darling Basin ecosystems and for downstream users have had to challenge this perverse ethic, arguing that their water flows are vital and productive. But at the same time, the system established to achieve greater environmental flows risks reinforcing this mindset by targeting water flowing from farms back to rivers as a waste to be captured and put to productive use. It also downplays the strong potential for the Jevons paradox: the situation, common in energy efficiency programs, whereby savings – in the absence of absolute limits – are used to fuel business expansion and increased resource use in pursuit of profits. Unlike natural baselines, the naturalised logics of capitalism are rarely contested.

The same capitalist interpretation of waste underpins the idea that water should be freed from under-performing users such as rivers and allowed to flow via magnetic market forces towards "higher-value" users. This notion is paper-thin at best, flimsy make-believe at worst. Value refers here to how much money an actor can extract from a certain use at the time, given the economics of production. It does not include the benefits an option could provide for others, including local communities, landscapes or river systems. It does not include the costs ("externalities") imposed on others by a certain water use, including the actual wasting away of World Heritage wetlands downstream. And it does not include long-term declines in value and the related risk that investments (whether almond trees, irrigation infrastructure, coalmines or small towns) will become stranded assets as climate change intensifies.

Simons notes that climate change projections for the Basin are dire, but skips the detail, pointing instead to the "million-mile stare" that commonly comes over farmers when the topic is raised. This sense of climate change as a paralysing future threat obscures the fact that it is already here, inseparable from the contemporary problems she documents, such as drought, community stress and changing consumer preferences. The "reliable" snow melt that she suggests distinguishes the Murray and Murrumbidgee rivers from those in the Northern Basin is already unreliable. The average rainfall and stream-flow figures that she uses to explain the Basin are already falling. These declines are unfolding not smoothly but jerkily, as abrupt step changes. Shifts in the timing of rainfall from cooler to warmer seasons mean that stream flow is vanishing far more quickly than the rainfall itself, and rain is increasingly arriving in short, sharp, damaging bursts. The impacts on river and stream systems are being compounded by concurrent climatic extremes and disasters, including the recent bushfires that, combined with floods and land clearing, have polluted dwindling water supplies. This includes urban water supplies – a topic that Simons does not discuss in detail, but is another reason the Murray–Darling Basin, and coal and coal seam gas basins, cannot be left to profiteers. As people in many rural areas already know, drinking water cannot be taken for granted.

How much the climate will change depends on how much more greenhouse gas is expelled into the air. How serious the impacts of climate change are will depend also on how well we adapt. Locking in water-hungry, energy-intensive land uses that return little to local communities other than some short-term jobs is one of the daftest pathways on offer, but it seems to be the one that current policies support. The irony is that even in the absence of basic funding, more innovative, prosperous, equitable, democratic and regenerative approaches are being fostered in pockets across the Basin by broadminded farmers, Catchment Management Authorities and new organisations.

It seems inescapable, reading Simons' *Cry Me a River*, that a powerful subset of political interests is exploiting the Basin in more ways than one. Existing environmental water savings are a great achievement, but far below where they should be. The question is why. Simons rightly argues that the complexity of the Basin's challenges cannot be reduced to a simple blame game, but it is evident that a convergent set of interests keep reaping short-term profits from the Basin while others increasingly suffer. In theory, this is not about the dominance of certain agricultural sectors (for example, cotton and almonds) over others, because not only are these sectors diverse, but their power also rests on the "higher value" their commodities demand at the time. Indeed, today's privileged sectors are not immune to water being redirected from them to still "higher value" (wealthier) users. As Basin irrigators fighting coal seam gas are finding, the "waste" of most interest is unused resources, not pollutants or degradation. Those pushing water towards the wealthiest and largest users of the Basin seem entwined with those vaporising the Basin's future rainfall by aggressively supporting a high-emissions pathway. Clearly, the once-agrarian National Party and their corporate allies are involved in this. But complex horizontal schisms characterise the Basin on the ground, as well as at state and federal political levels. Perhaps the one consistency is that those who are gaining the most are the ones who fervently believe that such an outcome is natural. It is a disheartening conclusion, but it reveals the diversity of those cast aside and thus the many potential alliances that could be forged to help rescue the Basin from the double sentence of deepening exploitation and climate change.

Lauren Rickards

CRY ME
A RIVER

Correspondence

Stefano de Pieri

Finally: a comprehensive explanation of how the Murray–Darling Basin Plan is unfolding. Margaret Simons' essay is a handy manual for all those who care about the future of this country. She has given the reader a ball of string with which to enter the Murray–Darling labyrinth. But while "manual" suggests a dry, technical piece of writing, Simons also captures the raw, everyday reality of the people who live in the Basin or are affected by the Plan.

I have lived and worked in north-west Victoria, on the Murray, for almost thirty years. In that time I have witnessed floods and droughts, the steady decline of inflows (no doubt attributable to climate change), the disappearance of small farms and the corporatisation of agriculture, and the transformation and shrinking of rural politics at the federal level, where "rural" and "regional" now mean de facto opposition to any sensible reforms. I have also witnessed the retreat of the ALP, a party to which I once belonged, from any form of regional involvement. Country Labor, whatever there was of it, has vanished. All policies now emanate from Canberra or the metropolitan centres. This is most evident in the bush. Here, only genuine independents voice alternative views. Some have received tacit support from the ALP, but mostly the ALP regards them as a sideshow. Except when they matter, as during Gillard's term in office.

Margaret asserts near the beginning of her essay that the ALP cannot win government without engaging with the regions, especially those where water plays a fundamental role. She says it almost in passing, and it is supported by a statement by me that she quotes towards the end of the essay. Phillip Adams failed to pick up on this point when talking with Margaret on *Late Night Live*; so did other interviewers. It made me suspect they had not read the essay fully. How else could such a big assertion be missed?

Labor needs a grand reform vision, both as a way to replace the confused conservative government (which abandoned all its economic theories overnight during the COVID-19 crisis) and as a roadmap for what it might achieve in power. The vision should be based on the fact that the cities and regions are interdependent. Historically, the Nationals have hijacked one half of this equation, arguing that the city owes the country. This is an essential part of the larger ideological apparatus behind the often supine Coalition partner. It is regularly used to bash moderate members, especially when it comes to climate and energy policies. The Nationals are magisterial in talking up their myths: that farmers produce food and fibre for the nation and the world, which entitles them to a seat at the government table, where they can shape policies in their own image and, above all, for their convenience. They have been at that game forever. It might have served country people well in the past, but today, with corporate agriculture taking over vast swathes of production, the word "farmer" means something else, and we all have a stake in the consequences.

The Nationals have become the toys of the coal industry and large corporations. The damage this has inflicted on this country is incalculable. It has happened in full view. While the media report on individual National stupidity, drunkenness or other shenanigans, less attention is paid to that fact that together with the hard right of the Liberal Party, they have run the nation into a hopeless cul-de-sac on water and energy.

In the absence of the ALP, the task of providing a contrast to the Nationals on almost every vital issue – from water and conservation to food security – has fallen to the Greens. Simons notes in her essay that Maryanne Slattery, formerly of the Authority, has supported dairy farmers and others who hate the Plan and want to see it "paused," if not repealed. I imagine Slattery reasons that since things cannot get any worse, why not mobilise the discontent against the Nationals, who are responsible for the mismanagement of our rivers, especially in New South Wales. That is clever politics. The Institute is led by Ben Oquist, former adviser to Bob Brown. To me, it looks like a manoeuvre of last resort and I am left to wonder what monsters might be born of populist support for the Shooters and Fishers!

Can the ALP shift its focus just enough from whatever it is currently running on (or from) to include vital environmental policies? Could agriculture and country life be managed by healthy, well-looked-after, smart regional communities? Could the ghastly, outdated, but still evident, ideological gap between cities and country finally be bridged?

Such an expansive, democratic vision might start by honestly interrogating whether it is necessary to compromise and damage our waterways, the lifeblood of biodiversity, to produce such a vast quantity of food – far more than we need.

Are a few billion dollars' worth of exports, especially cotton, worth the degradation of 70,000 kilometres of river? There is no imperative to produce food and fibre for the world, just as there is no imperative to produce coal. Our primary goal should be to maintain healthy environments where communities can thrive with an agreed quantity of water use in a manner that is beneficial to people and nature.

To ensure sustainable use, all water diversions should be measured in real time. Who knows what such an exercise would reveal about current water allocations? Then water trading should be modified, so that it is not only those with deep pockets who can survive in tough times. Surely there are scientists and economists who could design a revised trading system that, through genuine community consultation, could achieve the twin goals of environmental health and equity. In exchange for curbing the over-extraction of water, communities could be given much more generous funds for transport, education and health. At the moment, massive water use in agriculture generates profits for foreign entities, creating a false sense of wealth in river communities.

At this critical time, it is a concern that the shadow minister for agriculture is Joel Fitzgibbon, whose defence of coalmining after Labor's loss at the last election was proposed as a solution for regional areas. It is also a worry that some in the ALP argued publicly during the recent election post-mortem that the party should concentrate only on city seats. This would see Labor miss the opportunity to reinvigorate itself through active engagement with regional communities.

Of the three Southern Basin states, perhaps only Victoria has the critical environment necessary for developing such policies and feeding them to federal Labor. NSW water management is still in the same hopeless hands as ever, and South Australia's current Liberal government has no vigour. The states play a major role in water management and determine a lot of what happens on the ground. I cannot see how a narrow victory by the ALP at the next federal election – if there is a victory – could be lasting and robust without genuine engagement with the regions on water management. How can one govern when a large chunk of the productive population is not included in your vision, a population that lives on the very sites, in or out of the Basin, that are the cause of so much national division and pain?

Stefano de Pieri

CRY ME
A RIVER

Correspondence

Peter Gell

South Australians have long been sensitive to the volume of water entering the state down the River Murray and the impact of eastern-state users on the resource. Taking a somewhat postmodern view of *Cry Me a River*, one might conjecture that an author brought up in Adelaide and holidaying in the South Australian Riverina would understandably be culturally challenged to advocate reducing the state's water allocation to relieve difficulties experienced in the eastern states. So Simons readily concludes that South Australia's secure allocation of 1850 gigalitres each year is based on the need to underwrite Adelaide's water supply, flush salt inflows, support livelihoods and notionally retain the Coorong, Lower Lakes and Murray Mouth in the same condition as when they were listed for conservation in 1985 under the Ramsar Convention.

Simons is strongly supportive of the Plan, which aims to redeem up to 3200 gigalitres each year from irrigators for environmental purposes, keeping the lower lakes fresh, at a cost of $13 billion, and applauds the Guide to the Plan as "internationally peer-reviewed, scientifically based, open and transparent." It is therefore surprising that Simons is unwilling to accept the results of an original, internationally peer-reviewed, scientifically based paper published in *Hydrobiologia* (2007), which posited that Lake Alexandrina was much influenced by seawater and had become more fresh over the last 2000 years. Instead, she privileges a 2009 SA government–commissioned report that reinterprets these original findings as evidence of a freshwater paleohistory.

The 2009 report did not provide any new data; nor did it scarcely acknowledge, let alone critique, the 2007 paper to justify the change in interpretation. A recent CSIRO review has since found that the SA report understated the influence of seawater. The most recent scientific evidence (from Sydney University), published in *Nature Scientific Reports*, has shown Lake Alexandrina to have been strongly influenced by the sea until at least 5500 years ago, and likely estuarine thereafter.

The 2009 report was posted on a state-government website without peer review and was cited in a SA government "factsheet" claiming that "diatoms found in 7000 years of sediments indicate the majority of Lake Alexandrina *was fresh water in all years*" (my italics). The Basin Authority's watering plan also cited the report rather than the original 2007 paper when planning for a fresh Lake Alexandrina. I presented the contradiction between the data and the new interpretation in a keynote address at a conference in Glasgow in 2012, and later published it in *The SAGE Handbook of Environmental Change*.

It is only now, more than ten years after the report appeared on the government website, that some attempt has been made to justify the revised interpretation. In the absence of any new data, advocates have fallen back on the 1985 ecological character description to justify maintaining the lakes in a freshwater state, mistakenly believing that under the Ramsar Convention, Australia has an obligation to preserve the lakes in the state described at the time of listing. A past deputy secretary-general of Ramsar, in the peer-reviewed proceedings of an international conference, regarded this view as nonsense, because not all wetlands are pristine at the time of listing; such a determination would preclude nations from restoring sites should they wish; and it would effectively absolve all nations of the history of post-industrial degradation.

Simons' conversation with John Tibby concerning whether the research may have contributed to the Ramsar listing is both illogical, given the confusion in timing (listing 1985; publication 2007), and nonsensical, as the description can be changed and Australia's obligation is to the listing criteria, largely based on waterbirds and fish, rather than a character as described at a point in time.

The principal edict of the Ramsar Convention is the wise use of all wetlands. It would never be the intent of the convention to demand that a nation invest $13 billion to recover 3200 gigalitres of water from irrigation communities to enable a government to adhere rigidly to a character description written in 1985 and based on limited data. A change in listed ecological character can be sought at any time by the Australian government – with the support of the South Australian government. And there's the rub: while many nations have changed site-character descriptions, such support seems unlikely, as South Australia has amply demonstrated its enthusiasm for the 1985 description.

Under a drying climate and rising seas, it is inevitable that at some point Australia will have to relent on the commitment to a fresh Lake Alexandrina. When it does, we can remove the stake in the sand that says South Australia is entitled to 1850 gigalitres each and every year and begin to adopt basin-scale adaptation pathways to a different future. This may entail treating salt loads at source rather than running the river as a drain, reinstating natural estuarine variability and allowing for the daily rise and fall of the tides, providing for threatened fish that do not prefer their water to be fresh, and looking for other sources of water to avert catastrophic acidification upon the next drought. Yes, the Murray–Darling Basin is a tragedy; its rehabilitation will require us to envisage a sustainable future for all the people and environments in the Basin, and may require communities to give up some of the endearing lifestyles that hold people to place, for climate change will bring challenges that require Basin-scale thinking and multilateral cooperation.

Peter Gell

CRY ME
A RIVER

Correspondence

Jason Alexandra

I read Margaret Simons' essay while isolating on our horticultural farm in Gippsland. To the north, the Basin's headwaters snuggle into the folds of the Great Dividing Range; to the south is the massive Southern Ocean, source of frequent storms bringing us life-giving rains. As a farmer, I know the "magic" of irrigation – its productive power. I also love rivers, having devoted decades of my working life to restoring their health.

Simons offers many valuable insights into the byzantine relationships at the heart of Australia's water politics. There is the mind-numbing complexity of the technocratic rules and reform agreements, with the incessant reviews and inquiries. She explains well how the ritualised consultations have failed to bridge the deep discord, tensions and disconnections between national policies and local concerns, despite an "average of more than one meeting a day" somewhere in the Basin, according to the Murray–Darling Basin Authority's CEO.

I am deeply familiar with what Simons describes, but after more than thirty years working on water policy, the essay left me with a visceral, gut-wrenching sense of despair. What kind of nation does this to its rivers – repeatedly promising to restore them, yet failing to do so? And will this river crisis become a crisis of Federation – with High Court challenges looming?

During dull autumn weather, I mulled over this response. Crows raided the ripening fruit as the pickers gently stripped the orchard. I was sad and cranky. Like my former colleague at the Authority, Bill Johnson, I was grieving what we are losing. Not just the magnificent wetlands, like the Macquarie Marshes, once teeming with life, and the rivers, rich in fish and meaning, but also our collective faith in Australia's "can-do" approach to complex public policy. Surely, I thought, we can do better? But then I asked: where are the grounds for optimism?

Simons suggests we can find some hope in the Basin's vastness, the diversity of local initiatives and the separate evolution of the states' water-management cultures – the more conservative southerners contrasting with the cavalier north, where cotton is king. She points out the substantive differences between the Darling and the Murray and describes the raw politics governing who gets what they want. There is little doubt that pro-irrigation interests have captured most of the water, the regulators and the public purse, cementing their influence over the precious waters of this drying continent. The Basin illustrates what Nugget Coombs described as a reverse lottery, where a few people win a little bit and everybody else loses a lot.

One of the Basin's tragedies is that we have squandered a once-in-a-generation opportunity for critical reforms. Many structural problems remain unresolved, despite more than $20 billion spent on these reforms. According to the Productivity Commission's estimates, this far exceeds the market value of all the Basin's water entitlements. In this "user pays" era, no other sector has had such lavish treatment, yet many irrigators continue to complain, and noisily. However, no amount of money or protest will rectify the desiccating catchments, the declining inflows and the decreasing pool of water to share (as explained clearly in the recent Keelty report). A drying climate intensifies water conflicts. The maths is simple: there's more demand and less water with which to fulfil it. There are disruptive transitions occurring in the Basin involving people's lives and livelihoods. These are difficult and must be handled carefully. There are winners and losers.

Simons explains that the Murray–Darling Basin Plan has become a "lightning rod" for rural dissent. Codifying many pre-existing policies, like water markets, the Plan is the latest incarnation in a litany of inter-governmental agreements. In the 1994 COAG Water Reforms and the 2004 National Water Initiative, the state governments made ambitious promises about environmental flows (to be based on the best available science). Repeated failures to honour these commitments led to the Commonwealth interventions during the millennium drought.

Even with all the angst and the billions expended, the Plan may be consigned to history as yet another failure – perhaps simply too little, too late in a drying climate. Its success depends on the Commonwealth maintaining the political will and capability to regulate the states. To date, there is little evidence of this.

The Basin's fundamental problem – the over-extraction of water – has been apparent for decades. In 1995, on the banks of the Darling at Pooncarie, Victorian premier Joan Kirner launched a special edition of the Australian Conservation Foundation's journal *Habitat* – "The Darling: A river running out of time." The contributions by Indigenous activist Badger Bates, Timothy Fisher (later Penny Wong's water adviser) and me highlighted the dire consequences of expanding irrigation and floodplain harvesting upstream. Frighteningly, almost everything we warned about has transpired. Our efforts were then part of a broad-based coalition advocating a better deal for rivers, built on the successful Landcare alliance between the ACF and the National Farmers' Federation. Unfortunately, recent attempts to resurrect this consensus approach have gained little support due to the increasing polarisation and toxicity of Australia's water politics.

Climate change is exacerbating the impacts of over-extraction. As a senior executive for the Murray–Darling Basin Commission, and the Authority, between 2008 and 2013, I ran a significant risk-assessment program. We quantified the problems outlined by Simons – floodplain harvesting, climate change and reduced return flows. Unfortunately, the Plan's wafer-thin risk-management section uses none of the findings.

For decades, science has repeatedly warned that climate change is the most significant threat to the Basin's water resources, but the Plan comprehensively understates the climate risks and responds poorly to them. This is despite the *Water Act* requiring the MDBA to prepare a Plan that adjusts water use to the drying climate. South Australia's royal commissioner, Bret Walker, found that the Authority failed dismally in discharging this responsibility. Inconceivably, given the weight of evidence, the Plan projects historical averages forward. Hostile climate politics and rabid climate denialism condemned any opportunity for serious climate adaptation. ANU historian Daniel Connell describes it as governments gambling against the climate and losing.

Debates about the Basin's flows and climate always involve complex calculations and experts arguing about detailed models. While accurate figures are critically important, Simons' essay leaves the impression that something deeper is rotten in the relationship between our nation and its rivers – a corrosive malaise, fuelled by cynical politics, is eroding our ability to act collectively, to commune and therefore to govern. A plague of duplicity, "doublespeak" and "blame-shifting" cripples the integrity of the Basin's governance. There is constant fiddling with the numbers – creative water accounting. Without Maryanne Slattery's tireless work in making these numbers transparent and public, few outsiders could understand them. In her work with the Australia Institute, she has helped expose how government spending has resulted in massive wealth transfers to some irrigators, with questionable public benefits.

Only a few stalwarts believe the reforms are working. Little in Simons' essay provides hope for further substantive reform. Instead, many seem to have a dull acceptance that the best we can hope for is more tinkering with a broken system. Emblematic of this prevailing attitude is the concerning analogy used by the Authority's CEO, Phillip Glyde. He described the Basin's governance as "a really beat-up car that's almost dead, and that we are trying to upgrade it as we're driving it." Governing the Basin is not and will never be akin to repairing or using any machine – it's way more complicated. It requires navigating networks of human and institutional relationships and is therefore fundamentally social and intrinsically political.

As someone who has made my living as a farmer, environmental advocate and government executive, I am disturbed by the deepening divisions, declining optimism and lack of ambition for more just and accountable governing of the Basin. There is one certainty: governments and communities will continue arguing over these rivers. Therefore, we need inclusive, meaningful and productive negotiations, not more excuses, obfuscations, delays and blame-shifting. In this slowly unfolding national tragedy, I await anxiously the next act. I hope for some redemption – for the rivers and their people. However, regrettably, I fear the news will keep getting worse. I hope this fear is groundless.

Jason Alexandra

CRY ME A RIVER

Correspondence

R. Humphrey Howie

It's 12 April 2020. I have just returned from walking at Plush's Bend, 4 kilometres downstream from Renmark on the River Murray in South Australia. Here, 68 megalitres of Commonwealth environmental water is currently being delivered through a Renmark Irrigation Trust (RIT) pipe to a series of adjacent lagoons. Life is returning. Multitudes of martins and swallows glide and dip across the water surface. Dotterels skip along the edge and ducks work their way across its length.

Plush's Bend has been a popular recreational spot with settler families for over 100 years. Before that, the area was populated by the Erawirung people. The many middens and scar trees are reminders that they lived here for thousands of years. The rich riverine landscape, with its myriad creeks, billabongs and tributaries, was one of the most densely populated areas in Australia before European contact. In recent times, the lagoons at Plush's Bend have suffered from drastic water shortages, due to the infrequency of floods and high rivers. The large redgums are all dead, as are many of the box trees on the terraces above. However, in the second year of environmental watering, natural regeneration of native vegetation is occurring. This modest example demonstrates the critical value of the Murray–Darling Basin Plan. Returning water for environmental purposes from an over-allocated system is one of its principal aims.

Margaret Simons' essay is a lucid snapshot of where the Basin stands today. Through her many interviews, astute observations and evocative descriptions, she has captured the complexities of Australian politics, geography and culture with non-judgmental empathy. The vastness of the Basin means it is easy for communities to become insular. Her essay helps us connect with others living within the catchment.

My passion for the complex river landscape surrounding Renmark started early. Some of my fondest memories are of family outings swimming and picnicking at the Plush's Bend sandbar, or of our father taking us fishing in a dinghy among the snags and roots of overhanging gums. I have a vivid memory of returning from one of these expeditions as a teenager in the late 1970s. Dad and I were driving along a dusty track across the expansive Chowilla floodplain, about forty kilometres upstream of Renmark. Vast numbers of dead and dying black box trees were silhouetted in the failing light. After decades of diminishing high rivers and floods, they were finally giving up.

My dad could remember Lock 5 being constructed when he was a young lad, in 1927. After labouring on the fruit block, he would spend his spare time swimming, camping, fishing and hunting. Back then, the floodplain still had regular cycles of wetting and drying. Later, when Dad was a hard-working fruit grower and irrigator scarred by war, the river and its surrounds were his solace. After all that time, to see those floodplains dying was a tragedy that affected him deeply.

Fortunately, the Chowilla floodplain has not been forgotten: it was one of the six Icon sites identified in the 2002 Living Murray restoration program. Money and water have been allocated to rehabilitate the wetlands, redgum forests and 20 per cent of the original area of black box vegetation. Environmental watering and floodplain rehabilitation have begun.

Closer to the township of Renmark, environmental water is being delivered via the RIT to areas of the adjacent floodplain that can be reached by piped infrastructure. There are now eight active sites, with another seven to be commissioned. Simons described these efforts as "surprisingly crude," with "a piece of PVC pipe sticking out of the sand" – hardly "natural." In some ways, she is correct. However, we are only at the beginning, and still learning how best to irrigate the floodplain. As unnatural as delivering water through a "plumbed landscape" may seem to someone unfamiliar with the process, we expect it to achieve outcomes that are similarly beneficial environmentally to natural flooding events. While we cannot replicate high river or flooding events, connection of many of the sites can be achieved with less water.

Real benefits have already been observed after only two years. Along with significant vegetation regeneration, multitudes of birds and frogs are returning, including Australia's rarest waterfowl, the freckled duck. There has been amelioration of salinity-affected areas and importantly for RIT irrigators, the pipes are being flushed out, resulting in fewer blockages in on-farm filtration systems. The simple PVC pipe sticking out of the ground represents many years of hard work and goodwill among agencies required to initiate such a visionary, progressive project.

The project is administered by the Renmark Environmental Watering Committee, comprising representatives from the RIT, local government, government and non-government agencies, the Commonwealth Environmental Water Office, wetland ecologists and volunteers. The Committee has submitted detailed management plans to the Commonwealth Environmental Water Holder, necessary for the start of rehabilitation of the greater floodplain landscape surrounding the Renmark township. A great deal of research has gone into the project, it has a lot of support, and it is monitored closely.

Renmark was established by the Chaffey brothers and, with Mildura, is the oldest irrigation settlement in the country. Since 1887, it has supplied a diverse range of agricultural products to Australian cities and world markets, and consequently the floodplain landscape has absorbed the impacts of drainage, salinisation and logging for over 130 years. Environmental watering is perceived by some as a bit of a luxury. I believe this is because wetland and floodplain rehabilitation have never been valued adequately. The economic impact on agricultural production due to water being purchased for the environment can be quantified and consequently is often reported, but where are the metrics detailing the benefits to community wellbeing of having a healthy, rehabilitated landscape? How does one measure the educational reward for upcoming generations of studying floodplain management? Tourism and recreation opportunities are obvious economic advantages that have also been given little attention. In an egalitarian society, do we not have a responsibility to preserve our natural environment for all to enjoy, and to restore those parts of our world that have been damaged by our own misuse or neglect? How do you quantify the benefits of being in a healthy landscape for First Nations people and others who, like my father, endured mental and physical hardship? Ecological rehabilitation gives hope and social cohesion to communities. With our changing climate, this will become an absolute necessity.

Simons has achieved something rare. With her candid interviews, she has plunged into the complex workings of the Basin and rooted out core truths. She has detailed how the Plan was a bold and desperate attempt to address the chronic fundamental failings of the federal system and subsequent over-allocation of water. After many years in development, a figure for water buybacks was agreed upon which, in the end, pleased no one. Lack of scientific input, particularly of climate change modelling, is evident.

But despite widespread awareness of the Plan's shortcomings, few people are aware of the gains. Environmental watering has had some real benefits. Infrastructure spending on properties in return for water buybacks has been beneficial to irrigators. New technologies have been used in upgrading water distribution, establishing on-farm monitoring equipment, netting crops, valve control automation and developing telemetric meter reading. These technologies are allowing growers to adapt to an increasingly water-constrained future.

As Simons mentions, the Renmark Irrigation Trust was recently awarded platinum certification by the Alliance for Water Stewardship. The AWS was founded in Australia during the millennium drought of the early 2000s, and modelled on the international Forest Stewardship Council. AWS certification has steadily grown worldwide and major companies have signed on. Recognition was given to the Renmark Irrigation Trust for its strong governance, efficient water distribution and drainage network, community partnerships and, more latterly, floodplain rehabilitation strategy. Although it is early days, AWS certification has made the Renmark Irrigation Trust take stock of how far we have come and has given some metrics to this. It has highlighted risks to focus on. It has given members a voice when discussing policy with government agencies. Educational and professional institutions are expressing interest in partnerships. New possibilities and networks for produce marketing are opening up.

I believe wider adoption of AWS certification by Basin irrigators and communities will strengthen networks, increase collaboration and highlight common goals. Through these environmental initiatives and cooperation mechanisms, I feel hopeful that there is a bright future ahead. Maybe we can work towards evolving from a Basin society to a Basin community.

R. Humphrey Howie

CRY ME A RIVER

Response to Correspondence

Margaret Simons

Since *Cry Me a River* was released, people have asked me what should be done to fix the problems in the Murray–Darling Basin. It would be easy to protest that if the politicians and water bureaucrats can't solve the problem, it is wrong to expect a humble journalist to do so. Nevertheless, I agree with Gabrielle Chan, herself the author of impressive journalism on the Basin, that the numerous inquiries and reviews into the problems of the Basin have common threads, and that is the place to start. As Chan states, first there is the need for greater transparency. This should apply to who owns water and to water trades. When taxpayer money is spent on buying water, the reasons for the purchase, the price and the seller should be publicly disclosed. That, I would have thought, is neither a radical nor an unreasonable suggestion.

But there is a broader vibe about transparency. The acting chair of the Murray–Darling Basin Authority, Professor Stuart Bunn, talks about rebuilding trust – without saying how that trust was destroyed in the first place. Acts of radical transparency – around the research, the decision-making and the necessary compromises – are surely part of what is necessary. I accept the Authority has made some progress in its public communications. Much more is needed. Various grower groups will protest about commercial-in-confidence if water ownership is made transparent. I respond that in most states, if they sold land I would be able to find out what they sold, whether it was mortgaged and whom they sold it to – and probably for how much. Why should water be any different, particularly when it is a public asset, licensed to users?

What else? As Chan states, there are a number of reasons to suspect the efficiency schemes are not working as intended. There will be differences from place to place and scheme to scheme. Simple binaries will necessarily be wrong. But it seems that efficiency schemes and water trading are combining to increase the amount of land under irrigation. On top of this, if the return-flow figures are as dire as Quentin Grafton's work suggests, their net result might be to reduce the amount of water in the rivers – a counterintuitive but devastating outcome. It's awful that we don't already know the answer to the return-flow issue, and also that we don't know the quantum of floodplain harvesting and water kept in private storages in the Northern Basin. I think everyone agrees that priority must be given to improving our knowledge. It seems to me that it would be reasonable to pull back or even halt the spending on efficiency schemes at least until we know more.

As the Productivity Commission has suggested, the cheapest and surest way of clawing back water for the environment is for the government simply to buy it from willing sellers. I think history will conclude that Penny Wong was more right than wrong when, as water minister from 2007, she launched in with the government chequebook, without waiting for the Plan to be devised. It was a bold and imperfect action, but also effective. Nevertheless, I think that given the pain in rural communities, that effort shouldn't be repeated without a more comprehensive attempt to address the problems of agricultural industries and the communities that rely on them.

The Productivity Commission has pointed out that buybacks get blamed for broader problems in regional Australia, and also that there is not a one-for-one relationship between loss of water and decline in agricultural production. Farmers who have sold water adapt. They use what they have more efficiently, and may also move into dryland farming. If mass buybacks were reinstituted, it should be as part of comprehensive rural and regional policy. The money saved from the efficiency schemes could be spent on putting this policy into effect – probably including health and education spending in the regions, and perhaps also with attention given to essential services such as local news outlets, already the target of special government assistance. Such policy would intersect with education, health, food security, sovereignty and perhaps also migration policy, if we want to encourage new arrivals to settle outside the cities. In other words, water policy and regional policy needs a whole-of-government approach. It needs to be at the centre of the best of professional politics and rescued from the world of cynical compromise and ad-hoc side deals.

As the essay records, neither side of politics has come up with such policies.

I wish I had stated it more clearly in the essay: the National Party – which is almost always awarded water and agricultural portfolios at both state and federal level – has proved itself not up to the job. The party we might most expect to develop rural and regional policy has failed the test both in governance and integrity, and in policy smarts. The National Party has tied itself in knots. It is now hopelessly conflicted, trying to fend off the fury of the Southern Basin farmers – and their support for independent candidates and the Shooters, Fishers and Farmers Party – while staying in with the cotton farmers of the north. It would put the Nationals out of their misery if the water portfolios were taken from them – but of course that won't happen.

And the other parties don't come out of it well either. Since Malcolm Turnbull left the Water portfolio, the Liberal Party, particularly in New South Wales, has stood back while the National Party messed up the implementation. Labor, as de Pieri outlines, has, since it lost power federally, mostly failed to engage.

There are exceptions to the National Party's generally dismal record. It seems to me that former federal water minister David Littleproud did his best to manage the feral politics left by his predecessor, Barnaby Joyce, without surrendering policy integrity. When I finished *Cry Me a River*, it seemed there might have been a behind-the-scenes deal by Littleproud with Chris Brooks and the "Can the Plan" protesters to give them more water, using Mick Keelty's review as a cloak.

That didn't happen, and Littleproud held firm. Keelty's report, released in April 2020, contained few surprises for those in the know, finding that there was no spare water simply lying around to be re-allocated, that the reduction of inflows was the main reason for water allocations being reduced, and that part of the explanation for why Brooks and his fellows had no water, while their Victorian neighbours on the other side of the river had some, was because of different state government approaches to allocations – with New South Wales running the system hard, and with less in reserve to cope with dry seasons. Littleproud has now left the portfolio, replaced by the National Party's Keith Pitt, who oversaw another advance that could be seen as part of Littleproud's legacy – the NSW government's long-overdue lodgment of eleven of its water resource plans, with more to come.

The lodgment of those plans makes it apparent that the constant threats of NSW Nationals leader John Barilaro to pull out of the plan are nothing more than destructive showmanship, signifying nothing. Goodness knows why anyone thought Barilaro might be a good candidate in the federal seat of Eden Monaro. Southern NSW farmers would surely see right through him.

There have been other updates since *Cry Me a River* was published. The issue of the management of the lower lakes, and the status of Professor Peter Gell's work, has been settled by an independent CSIRO review of the science, which was underway when I wrote. That review concluded that the lakes were predominantly fresh before European settlement, and that they were being managed in accord with the best available science. In other words, no easy water savings there either. Gell has things to say about this in his correspondence – and to unpick it all he says would take more words than I have available here. I will let his suggestion that I am biased because I am South Australian travel through to the keeper. Those who are interested can access the CSIRO report on the Murray–Darling Basin Authority website. Professor Tibby's response to Gell's work is shortly to be published in the journal *Pacific Conservation Biology*, which also published the paper of Gell's that was so urgently pressed upon me by irrigators on the Murray.

In his correspondence, de Pieri wonders whether some of the political allegiances I outlined – such as the Australia Institute backing Chris Brooks and the Can the Plan protesters, who in turn have backed Shooters, Fishers and Farmers Party candidates – are "manoeuvres of last resort." In this context, it is notable that Maryanne Slattery, another of my correspondents, has now left the Australia Institute. I sense a story behind that – one for another time, maybe.

I think de Pieri writes the Shooters and Fishers off a bit lightly. They are a mixed bunch, both in talent and political lineage, and suffer from all the usual pathologies of minor parties – but the best of their candidates would be eligible in any party, and are well across water politics. They carry the legacy of the rural independents – Tony Windsor, in particular. The voters of southern New South Wales have not necessarily been wrong to ditch the National Party in their favour.

As I think my essay made clear, I don't necessarily share Slattery's positive view of Chris Brooks' contribution to water politics. As *Cry Me a River* records, Slattery herself has made an important contribution in bringing data on to the public record, in a climate of limited transparency from the authorities. And, granted, it is probably a good thing that it is now not only the cotton farmers of the Northern Basin who have a powerful political voice. Of course Brooks is within his democratic rights in giving voice to frustrated growers. But I don't think his interventions so far have moved much beyond special pleading, and some of what he has done has given his supporters false hope, which is not a kindness. This is not the kind of contribution that builds capacity to tackle the problems and build good policy. In fact, I think Brooks has made it harder to do that. I would say the same of some of the contributions of the cotton industry.

Meanwhile, "Can the Plan" is a near-meaningless slogan. What is the alternative to improving the Plan we have?

Slattery, Foran, Rickards and Howie, from varying standpoints, all draw attention to different kinds of non-financial value in a healthy river system. Foran, in particular, draws on clear expertise to delineate the complexities of water and cotton and the implications for those of us whose connection to the Basin is only through what we wear and what we eat. Howie teases out better than I had room to do the achievements of the Plan in environmental outcomes, perhaps going some of the way to addressing what Bunn sees as my shortcomings. Certainly, South Australia is one of the best advertisements for the work of the Commonwealth Environmental Water Holder, and not only because the success stories are easily accessible to the casual traveller. Rickards is eloquent about the experience of working in the Murray–Darling Basin Commission, and rightly draws attention to the role of water in mining and coal seam gas production – issues I couldn't tackle within my allocated word length. Beeson doesn't like my tone, suggesting that I fail to recognise the significance and complexity of the achievement in negotiating a flawed plan through parliament. Readers can judge for themselves on that, but as I said in *Cry Me a River*, it is a kind of miracle that we have a Plan at all. However, that fact shouldn't be used to dismiss serious problems in design and implementation. I agree with Beeson that the Plan is too important to fail, and Beeson agrees with me that the problems need to be part of wider policy debate. He emphasises water security. As I have already said, I would go broader.

The response from the Murray–Darling Basin Authority itself is submitted under the name of its acting chairman, Professor Bunn. As Mike Young elucidates, the fact that the MDBA has only an acting chair is part of the problem. The Authority has lacked a permanent chair since former Liberal MP Neil Andrew's term expired in early 2019 – at the same time as the South Australian royal commission's damning findings. The failure to recruit a permanent replacement is a lost opportunity, although one can understand that only the very brave would take on the job – that is, if they intended to do it well. Professor Bunn probably deserves credit he will never get for the thankless job of filling the gap.

Professor Bunn is a Griffith University academic with impressive credentials in water management. I found his response more remarkable for what it didn't say than what it did. He says nothing about the problems with efficiency programs, and nothing about the return-flows issue, for example, and nothing about the call for a water audit. After putting our problems in an international context, he suggests *Cry Me a River* was constructed as a kind of fairy story, or to meet some template journalistic story arc. Again, readers can judge for themselves, and I will strive not to feel insulted. On the positive side, Professor Bunn's response is remarkable for containing the clearest statement so far from the Authority that climate change "will undoubtedly require a revisit of the broader settings of the Plan." And he talks about 2026, when the current arrangements expire, as bringing about such a comprehensive reset.

Mike Young gave me a key interview at the beginning of my project, and I am relieved that he thinks I "got it so right." Certainly he would be the one to call me out if I had made errors!

Given Bunn's acknowledgment of climate change and the need for a reset of the Plan's fundamentals, it seems likely that Young's proposal for a "shares" system will get another run in 2026, if not before. Young's system seems to me to have a tough kind of fairness and flexibility built in, although, as he indicates, it would not allow us to escape from the hard realities that water inflows will decrease, and that means yet more hardship for rural communities – I would say increasing the need for broader policy responses.

There would still be plenty to argue about in putting a system such as Young suggests in place. What share should be reserved for the environment? What emphasis, if any, should be given to maintaining diversity in agriculture? Should compensation be paid for reductions in water shares for irrigators? And how much? But these are the arguments worth having. The problem with the sustainable diversion limit approach is that the complexities of understanding what water can be used by whom and when mean that is almost impossible for anyone to understand what is being done, let alone debate on the basis of clear data and sensibly argue for change.

Young and Slattery are unlikely to agree on much. He has faith in free markets. She argues for government intervention to protect values that are not only financial, such as food security and a diverse family farming sector. I won't choose between them, but it seems to me the debate over a shares system might provide a framework in which these issues can be worked through, as well as incorporating other policy objectives around decentralisation and food security.

I imagine de Pieri would have been heartened when, almost as though he had read this correspondence, Labor leader Anthony Albanese made regional policy a feature of his May headland speech, saying that an "appropriate decentralisation strategy which boosts regional economic development and takes pressure off our capital cities should be at the heart of national economic development." Albanese described a "once in a generation" chance to reshape our economy, including the possibility for businesses to move to the regions and money to be spent on river revitalisation. Of course, details were absent, but it is worth watching the space. If the 2022 election includes a contest over rural and regional policy, food security and resource management, that would surely be a good thing.

I also see some hope in the National Cabinet that has been created to address the COVID-19 crisis. If it persists after the immediate crisis has passed, surely one of the items on the top of its agenda should be the Murray–Darling Basin.

Perhaps it could move past the depressing theatrics and zero-sum politics of the Murray–Darling Basin Ministerial Council and CHOGM. Notably, the National Cabinet includes no National Party members.

Meanwhile, the government's response to the COVID-19 crisis has included a new emphasis on "sovereignty," including food supply chains and with fertiliser manufacture in Narrabri at the top of the list of projects being promoted by the National COVID-19 Coordination Commission. This, too, suggests that rural and regional policy might be brought back into the centre of politics, not left to neglect and the world of cosy conversations and opaque political compromise.

Margaret Simons

Jason Alexandra worked on Murray–Darling Basin policy for over thirty years, including five as a senior executive at the Basin Authority. He now runs an irrigation farm (orchards). His writing has been published by *The Conversation*, the ABC and the World Water Forum.

Geoff Beeson is an independent researcher and an honorary professor at Deakin University. He is the author of *A Water Story: Learning from the Past, Planning for the Future*.

Judith Brett is emeritus professor of politics at La Trobe University. A former editor of *Meanjin* and columnist for *The Age*, she won the National Biography Award in 2018 for *The Enigmatic Mr Deakin*. She is the author of three previous Quarterly Essays: *Relaxed and Comfortable*, *Exit Right* and *Fair Share*. Her other books include *From Secret Ballot to Democracy Sausage*, *Robert Menzies' Forgotten People* and *Australian Liberals and the Moral Middle Class*.

Stuart Bunn is the director of the Australian Rivers Institute at Griffith University and the acting chair of the Murray–Darling Basin Authority.

Gabrielle Chan has been a journalist for more than thirty years, covering politics for *The Australian* and *Guardian Australia*. In 1996, she moved to a sheep and wheat farm in south-west New South Wales. She is the author of *Rusted Off: Why Country Australia is fed up*.

Stefano de Pieri's acclaimed restaurant, Stefano's, is located in Mildura. He has published several cookery books, two associated with his ABC television series *A Gondola on the Murray*. He helped establish the Mildura Writers Festival and has had a long engagement with politics.

Barney Foran is an adjunct research fellow at the Institute of Land, Water and Society at Charles Sturt University, Albury. Previously, he worked for thirty years with CSIRO in physical economy analysis, futures and rangelands management.

Peter Gell is professor of environmental science at Federation University. He specialises in the use of diatoms as indicators of present and past river and lake conditions, particularly in coastal systems and across the Murray–Darling Basin.

R. Humphrey Howie is a fourth-generation fruit grower from Renmark, South Australia. He is the presiding member of the Renmark Irrigation Trust, which delivers water to 600 irrigator members. He is also chairman of the Renmark Environmental Watering Committee.

Lauren Rickards co-leads the RMIT Climate Change Transformations research program and is a lead author of the Intergovernmental Panel on Climate Change.

Margaret Simons is an award-winning journalist and the author of thirteen books, including biographies of Malcolm Fraser and Penny Wong. She won the 2015 Walkley Award for Social Equity Journalism and has been honoured with several Quill Awards for Journalistic Excellence.

Maryanne Slattery was a director of the Murray–Darling Basin Authority for over a decade before becoming senior water researcher at the Australia Institute. She is now a director of the water consultancy Slattery and Johnson.

Mike Young holds a research chair in Water and Environmental Policy at the University of Adelaide and was the founding director of its Environment Institute. Before joining the University of Adelaide, he spent thirty years with CSIRO.

QUARTERLY ESSAY BACK ISSUES

BACK ISSUES: (Prices include GST, postage and handling within Australia.) *Grey indicates out of stock.*

- ☐ **QE 1** ($15.99) Robert Manne *In Denial*
- ☐ **QE 2** ($15.99) John Birmingham *Appeasing Jakarta*
- ☐ **QE 3** ($15.99) Guy Rundle *The Opportunist*
- ☐ **QE 4** ($15.99) Don Watson *Rabbit Syndrome*
- ☐ **QE 5** ($15.99) Mungo MacCallum *Girt By Sea*
- ☐ **QE 6** ($15.99) John Button *Beyond Belief*
- ☐ **QE 7** ($15.99) John Martinkus *Paradise Betrayed*
- ☐ **QE 8** ($15.99) Amanda Lohrey *Groundswell*
- ☐ **QE 9** ($15.99) Tim Flannery *Beautiful Lies*
- ☐ **QE 10** ($15.99) Gideon Haigh *Bad Company*
- ☐ **QE 11** ($15.99) Germaine Greer *Whitefella Jump Up*
- ☐ **QE 12** ($15.99) David Malouf *Made in England*
- ☐ **QE 13** ($15.99) Robert Manne with David Corlett *Sending Them Home*
- ☐ **QE 14** ($15.99) Paul McGeough *Mission Impossible*
- ☐ **QE 15** ($15.99) Margaret Simons *Latham's World*
- ☐ **QE 16** ($15.99) Raimond Gaita *Breach of Trust*
- ☐ **QE 17** ($15.99) John Hirst *'Kangaroo Court'*
- ☐ **QE 18** ($15.99) Gail Bell *The Worried Well*
- ☐ **QE 19** ($15.99) Judith Brett *Relaxed & Comfortable*
- ☐ **QE 20** ($15.99) John Birmingham *A Time for War*
- ☐ **QE 21** ($15.99) Clive Hamilton *What's Left?*
- ☐ **QE 22** ($15.99) Amanda Lohrey *Voting for Jesus*
- ☐ **QE 23** ($15.99) Inga Clendinnen *The History Question*
- ☐ **QE 24** ($15.99) Robyn Davidson *No Fixed Address*
- ☐ **QE 25** ($15.99) Peter Hartcher *Bipolar Nation*
- ☐ **QE 26** ($15.99) David Marr *His Master's Voice*
- ☐ **QE 27** ($15.99) Ian Lowe *Reaction Time*
- ☐ **QE 28** ($15.99) Judith Brett *Exit Right*
- ☐ **QE 29** ($15.99) Anne Manne *Love & Money*
- ☐ **QE 30** ($15.99) Paul Toohey *Last Drinks*
- ☐ **QE 31** ($15.99) Tim Flannery *Now or Never*
- ☐ **QE 32** ($15.99) Kate Jennings *American Revolution*
- ☐ **QE 33** ($15.99) Guy Pearse *Quarry Vision*
- ☐ **QE 34** ($15.99) Annabel Crabb *Stop at Nothing*
- ☐ **QE 35** ($15.99) Noel Pearson *Radical Hope*
- ☐ **QE 36** ($15.99) Mungo MacCallum *Australian Story*
- ☐ **QE 37** ($15.99) Waleed Aly *What's Right?*
- ☐ **QE 38** ($15.99) David Marr *Power Trip*
- ☐ **QE 39** ($15.99) Hugh White *Power Shift*
- ☐ **QE 40** ($15.99) George Megalogenis *Trivial Pursuit*
- ☐ **QE 41** ($15.99) David Malouf *The Happy Life*
- ☐ **QE 42** ($15.99) Judith Brett *Fair Share*
- ☐ **QE 43** ($15.99) Robert Manne *Bad News*
- ☐ **QE 44** ($15.99) Andrew Charlton *Man-Made World*
- ☐ **QE 45** ($15.99) Anna Krien *Us and Them*
- ☐ **QE 46** ($15.99) Laura Tingle *Great Expectations*
- ☐ **QE 47** ($15.99) David Marr *Political Animal*
- ☐ **QE 48** ($15.99) Tim Flannery *After the Future*
- ☐ **QE 49** ($15.99) Mark Latham *Not Dead Yet*
- ☐ **QE 50** ($15.99) Anna Goldsworthy *Unfinished Business*
- ☐ **QE 51** ($15.99) David Marr *The Prince*
- ☐ **QE 52** ($15.99) Linda Jaivin *Found in Translation*
- ☐ **QE 53** ($15.99) Paul Toohey *That Sinking Feeling*
- ☐ **QE 54** ($15.99) Andrew Charlton *Dragon's Tail*
- ☐ **QE 55** ($15.99) Noel Pearson *A Rightful Place*
- ☐ **QE 56** ($15.99) Guy Rundle *Clivosaurus*
- ☐ **QE 57** ($15.99) Karen Hitchcock *Dear Life*
- ☐ **QE 58** ($15.99) David Kilcullen *Blood Year*
- ☐ **QE 59** ($15.99) David Marr *Faction Man*
- ☐ **QE 60** ($15.99) Laura Tingle *Political Amnesia*
- ☐ **QE 61** ($15.99) George Megalogenis *Balancing Act*
- ☐ **QE 62** ($15.99) James Brown *Firing Line*
- ☐ **QE 63** ($15.99) Don Watson *Enemy Within*
- ☐ **QE 64** ($15.99) Stan Grant *The Australian Dream*
- ☐ **QE 65** ($15.99) David Marr *The White Queen*
- ☐ **QE 66** ($15.99) Anna Krien *The Long Goodbye*
- ☐ **QE 67** ($15.99) Benjamin Law *Moral Panic 101*
- ☐ **QE 68** ($15.99) Hugh White *Without America*
- ☐ **QE 69** ($15.99) Mark McKenna *Moment of Truth*
- ☐ **QE 70** ($15.99) Richard Denniss *Dead Right*
- ☐ **QE 71** ($15.99) Laura Tingle *Follow the Leader*
- ☐ **QE 72** ($15.99) Sebastian Smee *Net Loss*
- ☐ **QE 73** ($15.99) Rebecca Huntley *Australia Fair*
- ☐ **QE 74** ($15.99) Erik Jensen *The Prosperity Gospel*
- ☐ **QE 75** ($22.99) Annabel Crabb *Men at Work*
- ☐ **QE 76** ($22.99) Peter Hartcher *Red Flag*
- ☐ **QE 77** ($22.99) Margaret Simons *Cry Me a River*

NAME:

ADDRESS:

EMAIL: PHONE:

Please include this form with payment details overleaf.

QUARTERLY ESSAY
CRY ME A RIVER
THE TRAGEDY OF THE MURRAY–DARLING BASIN
MARGARET SIMONS
Correspondence
'RED FLAG' Amy King, David Walker, John West, Richard McGregor, Henry Sherrell, Wanning Sun, Caroline Rosenberg, Sam Roggeveen, Peter Hartcher

QUARTERLY ESSAY
RED FLAG
WAKING UP TO CHINA'S CHALLENGE
PETER HARTCHER
Correspondence
'MEN AT WORK' Grant Marjoribanks, Maddison Connaughton, Angela Shanahan, Marian Baird, Andrew Wear, Mark Tennant, Andrew Thackrah, Annabel Crabb